Battleground Europe
MARKET GARDEN

ARNHEM
THE LANDING GROUNDS
& OOSTERBEEK

Battleground Europe
MARKET GARDEN

ARNHEM
THE LANDING GROUNDS
& OOSTERBEEK

Frank Steer

LEO COOPER

Published in 2002 and
reprinted in 2009 by
LEO COOPER
an imprint of
Pen & Sword Books Limited
47 Church Street, Barnsley, South Yorkshire S70 2AS

ISBN 978 0 85052 856 5

A CIP catalogue of this book is available
from the British Library

Printed by CPI UK

*For up-to-date information on other titles produced under the Leo Cooper
imprint, please telephone or write to:*
Pen & Sword Books Ltd, FREEPOST, 47 Church Street
Barnsley, South Yorkshire S70 2AS
Telephone 01226 734222

CONTENTS

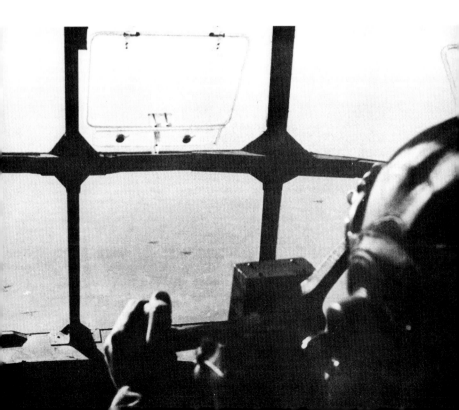

FOREWORD

I am delighted that I have been asked to write the foreword to this book.

Over the years, a great deal has been written about the battle of Arnhem in 1944. This has been mainly about the attempted capture of the bridge over the Rhine by the parachute battalions. Little attention by the media has ever been given to the men of the Air Landing Brigade. Those who too wore the red beret, but were given the task of defending the perimeter of the battle in an attempt to keep open the last ferry across the Rhine in the area of Oosterbeek. This was just as an important part of the battle as that for the bridge, for had the armour of the relieving forces not had this ferry and an area on the North side of the river to deploy in, their task would have been much harder.

As we all know the division was withdrawn before the armoured units arrived. It is to Brigadier Frank Steer that a great deal is now owed in writing this book which highlights the very intense battle which went on in the area of the suburb of Oosterbeek and in which many men lost their lives and many others were wounded. As an example, in my own company at the end of the battle there were only nine men left and one officer badly wounded who were still fighting on. The rest of the 110 strong company had either been killed or wounded. This was typical of the position along the whole perimeter. There were many acts of heroism in this area, most of which are unrecorded because men were killed or taken prisoner.

So, I commend this book and the tour of this part of the Arnhem battlefield to you.

Reverend Canon,
Alan Green
Leicester, May 2002.

PREFACE

In writing this guide to the landing areas used by the 1st British Airborne Division in its attempt to take the Arnhem Bridge, and in seeking to describe some of the fighting in and around Oosterbeek, a small town to the west of Arnhem, I have been fortunate to obtain the support of a number of authors, friends and colleagues. The result, I hope, is that visitors who have had limited opportunity to study this most complex operation will be able to have an enjoyable and informative visit to the area and gain a broad, clear understanding of this part of the battle.

Authors on Arnhem now face the fact that many of the participants who contributed to earlier works with their anecdotes are to a great extent no longer in a position to do so. Therefore, whilst I have been able to include original source material from my own studies of logistics at Arnhem, I have been to a great extent dependent upon fellow authors or their relatives to quote or use material from their works on the battle. They have given their permission willingly and without caveat and I am enormously grateful to them:

Christopher Hibbert from *Arnhem*; General Sir Anthony Farrar-Hockley from *Airborne Carpet: Operation Market Garden*; Stuart Eastwood, Charles Gray and Alan Green from *When Dragons Flew – An Illustrated History of the 1st Battalion The Border Regiment 1939-45*; Ron Kent from *First In! Parachute Pathfinder Company*; Robert Sigmond from *Off At Last – An Illustrated History of the 7th (Galloway) Battalion The King's Own Scottish Borderers 1939 – 1945*, John Fairley from *Remember Arnhem*; Robert J Kershaw from *It Never Snows in September*; John Waddy from *A Tour Of The Arnhem Battlefields*; Harry Bankhead from *Salute To The Steadfast – From Delhi To Arnhem With 151/156 Parachute Battalion*; Niall Cherry from *Red Berets and Red Crosses*; Peter Wilkinson from *The Gunners at Arnhem*; Stuart Mawson from *Arnhem Doctor*; and Mrs Pamela Urquhart From *Arnhem* by Major General Roy Urquhart. Without their agreement a work of this sort, so dependent on the experiences of those present to be meaningful, would simply never have got off the ground.

Drs Adrian Groeneweg OBE, vice-chairman of the board of trustees of the Airborne Museum Hartenstein was as ever on hand to provide guidance, support and help. He has been a friend and teacher for many years and his unfailing preparedness to help and advise is a constant refuge for those who wish to learn more of, and learn lessons from, the

8

events of September 1944. He knows he has my immeasureable thanks.

Dr Robert Voskuil was also unstinting in his assistance to my endeavour. Both were kind enough to spend time on my drafts and kind enough not to be too unkind about my errors, for which I am more than grateful. Robert Voskuil, as well as helping me with photographs from the late-war or immediate post-war period, went out of his way to obtain a number of the modern pictures that appear in the book. He also took the time to prove the route, checking that my directions made some sort of sense. I am encouraged that he found them both easy to follow and relevant. Robert Sigmond, always a source of wisdom and knowledge, provided additional material, and in particular photographs of KOSB soldiers. Jook and Hanna van Slooten's home was always a haven of peace and laughter where a weary researcher could find solace, a warm welcome and an endless supply of quite excellent tea. Jook's help and guidance with local information and proof reading were invaluable, and I am grateful to him and Hanna also for checking the routes and confirming the detail of some of the distances quoted.

I would like to thank the Trustees of the Airborne Forces Charities Trust for their kind permission to reproduce the painting, *Arnhem 1944* by Lea, on the front cover.

I am immensely grateful to Alan Green for reading the draft of this book and for providing the foreword. He, after all, was there and knows what it was really like, far better than any of us who try to represent events now half a century old. We have walked his battle ground together and he has my respect in great measure; as have all those who were at Arnhem. His approval of what I have tried to encapsulate in this small guide to one part of Operation MARKET GARDEN means more than I can express in words.

To all of those who helped, my thanks and the hope that I have taken proper account of all your points. If I have been unsuccessful then any mistakes are my responsibility and mine alone.

Brigadier Frank Steer MBE
Kent, 2002.

GLOSSARY

ACC	Army Catering Corps
CO	Commanding Officer
COMPO	Composite Rations
Coy	Company
CWGC	Commonwealth War Graves Commission.
DAA	Divisional Administrative Area.
DUKW	A two and a half ton, 6X6 amphibious vehicle. D – 1942; U – Amphibious; K – 6x6 Drive; W – Tandem.
DZ	Dropping Zone.
HQ	Headquarters.
KOSB	King's Own Scottish Borderers.
LZ	Landing Zone.
Mortar	Infantry battalions' artillery. Bomb range around 3,000 yards.
NCO	Non-Commissioned Officer.
OFP	Ordnance Field Park
PIAT	Projector Infantry Anti-Tank.
RAF	Royal Air Force.
RAMC	Royal Army Medical Corps.
RAOC	Royal Army Ordnance Corps.
RAP	Regimental Aid Post.
RASC	Royal Army Service Corps.
RE	Royal Engineers.
RV	Rendezvous

SIZE AND SHAPE

To help understand the story there follows a short description of the size and shape of the military formations mentioned in the book:

Corps:

A grouping of divisions, typically between two and four. Size between 30,000 (a light airborne corps) and 50,000 (a full all-arms structure) men with, in the latter case, some 25% of the total strength comprising corps level units (logistics, artillery, engineers). Commander – Lieutenant General.

Division:

A grouping of brigades, typically between two and four, together with a number of divisional level units (logistics, artillery, engineers) making up some 25% of the total strength. Size between 10,000 (airborne) and 25,000 (all-arms) men. Commander – Major General.

Brigade:

A grouping of battalions, usually three, plus a very limited number of brigade level units making up perhaps 10% of the total strength. Size between 2,500 (airborne) and 5,000 (all-arms) men. Commander – Brigadier.

Battalion:

A grouping of companies, three or four. Some 40% of a battalion would be in the support element (heavy weapons, logistics, engineering, administration). Size between 700 and 900. Commander – Lieutenant Colonel.

Company/Squadron:

A grouping of three or four platoons/troops. Size between 100 and 120, although some specialist units would be smaller. Commander – Major

Platoon:

A grouping of sections, almost always three. Size between twenty-six and thirty-five. Commander – Lieutenant or Second Lieutenant.

Section:

A group of between 8 and 10 men, commanded by a corporal.

ADVICE FOR VISITORS

A visit to the scene of the battle fought between 17 and 26 September 1944 by the 1st British Airborne Division in its attempt to reach and hold the road bridge over the Lower Rhine at Arnhem in the Netherlands, takes the visitor to a number of villages lying a few miles to the west of Arnhem itself: principally Oosterbeek, Renkum, Wolfheze and Heelsum. Lying in the eastern part of the Netherlands and not far from the German border, it is a delightful part of a delightful country.

The countryside around the villages has changed very little since 1944. Of course, there are more buildings, and the huge advances in public facilities and transport that are a mark of Dutch investment in their country are clear for all to see. However, the lie of the land remains as it was: largely open farmland interspersed with areas of forest and heath land; and trenches can still be found in the woods through which some of the fighting took place. It is a wealthy area, as it was before the war. The houses tend to be large, with imposing gardens interspersed by chain link fences and hedges that presented enormous problems to friend and foe alike during the battle.

The weather is variable, with similar maritime influences to our own climate. However, on a really hot summer's day wisdom does suggest cream and a hat to ward off the sun. The ground is flat and the soil sandy and well drained, with only a few small hills to walk up. This tour does not, therefore, require robust walking boots, but comfortable cross-country shoes will be helpful. There are a reasonable number of watering holes on this tour, so in the event of rain it should be relatively easy to find shelter. However, a light waterproof is also a good idea in case you stray a little way from the car, although provisions, such as flasks of tea are, really, unnecessary.

Health insurance, accompanied by an E111 (available from post offices on production of a national insurance number), is strongly recommended.

To get to the area the alternatives involve either ferries or flying. As to ferries, Dover to Calais is the shortest crossing, using either P&O Stena or Sea France. The P&O Stena sailings are very much more frequent, but it is worth checking both company's tariffs to see what special deals they are offering. Driving sensibly and given good traffic the centre of Arnhem, just 6 to 8 miles to the east of the battlefield tour area, is under four hours from Calais, and all the motorways are toll free. The timing allows for one stop, on the Dutch/Belgian border at Breda. To get to Breda, follow the E40/A16 from the port of Calais to Dunkirk, on to Ostend and then to Brussels. In the area of Ghent you reach the junction with the E17 and turn north towards Antwerp. Once at the Antwerp Ring Road the signs for Breda are obvious and you follow them to your comfort stop at the motorway rest area. On departure from Breda, drive north on the motorway A58 and then the A27/E311 in the direction of Utrecht until its junction with the A15. Turning onto the A15/E31 follow it east, signed Nijmegen. Once beyond Tiel and before Nijmegen there are two choices, and the one you select may well depend on where you may be staying. If you are lodging in the town of Arnhem you should follow the signs to Nijmegen and Arnhem and go into the town across the motorway bridge into Arnhem. For those staying in or around Oosterbeek, however, turn north at the junction with the motorway A50 signed Apeldoorn and at the second junction, having just crossed the Rhine, turn off and follow the signs for Oosterbeek.

For those in the north and east of the UK, Harwich or Hull may be better departure ports, travelling to the Hook or Rotterdam/Europort respectively. From either of these ferry terminals the A15 is easy to find and follow and the driving time is under two hours.

By air, there are flights to Schipol, Amsterdam's airport, from most UK main and regional airports. Once there either hire a car, or take the train from the station at the airport, and with one change it takes you to Arnhem. Please note, however, three of the four tours in this guide require a motor car, so hiring in some form will be necessary if you choose to fly or take the train.

Driving in The Netherlands carries few surprises. Roads are wide and good, but do beware at roundabouts where they have some differences on rights of way although the general rule is that all traffic, including bicycles and horse riders from the right, has right of way. Guidance, if unsure, can be obtained from your motoring organisation. The Oosterbeek area has a number of dense woods, and where roads pass through them you are invited to use dipped headlights as a warning to oncoming motorists; and driving lit up everywhere is officially recommended.

As a pedestrian do watch out for the cycle tracks. They usually stand out, being of red tarmac surfacing, but not always. However, there is a tendency by the uninitiated to use them as footpaths or pavements, which they are not. The cyclist has right of way, although they will usually try to warn with a bell. However, do take care to look both ways when venturing near one.

As to maps, any standard continental road atlas available at main bookstores or through the motoring organisations will suffice as a guide to get you there. Once in the area any bookshop or petrol station will sell good quality local area street and road maps that will be more than adequate for a good and detailed tour. If you are unsure about your purchase covering the whole area of the battle simply ask and the shopkeeper or garage attendant is almost certain to be able to advise.

During your visit to the Netherlands communication will not be a problem. If those you address in English cannot speak the language then they are probably not Dutch. You will find the people of Oosterbeek, Wolfheze, Renkum and Heelsum have a very special relationship with their British guests, and especially those who were either present at the battle or members of their families. You will be received with friendliness unequalled anywhere in the world – it is a truly remarkable experience, and is built on a relationship that promises to endure for a long time to come.

As to accommodation, Arnhem is a good place in which to stay as a base for this tour. As a guide, the Haarhuis (0031 26 4427441; email haarhuis@bart.nl) is a four star Best Western Hotel, whilst the Old Dutch (0031 26 4420792) is a smaller, but very comfortable, establishment just up the street. Both are directly opposite the railway station – and following the road signs to 'Station' makes them very easy to find. They are conveniently positioned for the centre of the town with its plethora of bars, pubs and restaurants, all offering excellent service and good value for money.

If, however, you wish to be closer to Oosterbeek and the landing areas then the West-End Hotel is a good choice. The address is:

Amsterdamseweg 505, 6816 VK Arnhem.

Email: receptie@westend.valk.com,

telephone 0031 26 4821100 or fax 0031 26 4821614

For those wishing to camp or caravan then there is a well-signed site in Oosterbeek near the sports ground and it is shown in all good caravan site guides. Details of other accommodation, and information on other related issues, can be obtained from the Tourist Information office in Oosterbeek: Telephone 0031 26 3333172 or Fax 0031 26 3332990. They can also put you in touch with the Arnhem office, which has better resources.

There are four tours described in this guide, one on foot and three by car, and it is perfectly possible to complete them all in one day, albeit a long day. However, a visit to the Airborne Museum Hartenstein, which was the headquarters of the 1st British Airborne division during the battle, is a must and preferably at the start of your tour. The museum, though, is only open between 10.00 am and 5.00 pm Monday to Saturday between 1 April and 1 November, and 11.00 am to 5.00pm for the rest of the year. On Sundays and public holidays timings are 12.00 midday to 5.00 pm. Timing is, therefore, difficult, but if it can be visited the day before that would be best. It has a wonderful range of exhibits and its diorama of the battle offers a very clear explanation of what happened and will assist greatly in understanding what was a very complex operation. Attention span in museums differs widely from person to person, but a minimum of an hour should be allocated to the Hartenstein for a proper overview of events. Each of the tours in this guide commences at one of the car parks near the museum.

The Hartenstein is easily reached by turning south off Utrechtseweg just 100 metres west from the crossroads with Stationsweg and Pietersbergseweg in Oosterbeek. Just as you turn left off Utrechtseweg there is a large church on the left where the car park is usually reserved for coaches. With a car take the first right and park behind the Kleyn Hartensteyn Café from where it is a 200 metre walk to the museum.

Your tour will be more fruitful if you can read this guide before departure. It will help put into context what happened and will serve as a useful reference as you drive into and around the area. Arnhem was a hugely complex battle, with a number of key events overlapping, and with two battles really taking place: one in Arnhem itself and the other in Oosterbeek. This guide does not set out to cover every single aspect of what happened, or cover every event in detail. It seeks to offer visitors an overview, and to allow them to obtain a real feel for events without becoming overburdened with a plethora of detailed information which only the most well-informed could assimilate, and which is covered in the many books on this battle.

Once on the spot in Oosterbeek this guide will describe what happened, using, wherever possible, anecdotes from veterans. After

The Airborne Museum 'Hartenstein'.

15

all, it is they who were there and without their input a work of this sort is without colour. Wherever ranks are used they refer to those held during the battle and do not reflect any advancement which might have been subsequently achieved in a post-war military career.

Try, if you can, as you read the text in the privacy of your home or out on the battlefield, to imagine a gallant, and now very old, gentleman wearing a blazer, his regimental tie and a red beret, his medals displayed proudly above his left breast pocket, speaking gently as he tells you of a time of unimagined horror and inexplicable courage – and forgive him, please, the tear in his eye as he remembers what happened in those dark days and those who were with him then in body, and who remain with him in spirit.

A Horsa Glider. Courtesy Museum of Army Flying.

CHAPTER ONE

OPERATION MARKET GARDEN

The Plan in Outline

The Allied armies that had invaded Europe across the Normandy beaches on 6 June 1944 had broken the German Army in France by early August. By 25 August they had entered Paris, by 3 September Brussels had been liberated. Everywhere, great armies were pushing the Germans back to their own borders. However, the Allies had not been successful in capturing the Channel ports. All supplies had to come across the invasion beaches or through Cherbourg, the latter having been severely damaged and lying some 400 miles from the forward fighting elements. This all created a significant logistic challenge, and impacted severely on the ability of commanders to conduct effective operations. The British capture of Antwerp on 4 September should have made all the difference, but did not go far

The German Army had suffered what were considered by the Allies to be crippling defeats. 'It would all be over by Christmas.'

enough. Major General Roberts' 11th Armoured Division captured the port itself, as he had been instructed to do, but did not pursue the Germans onto and beyond the north bank of the River Scheldt. By allowing the Germans to retain their domination of the north bank Antwerp's use as a port was denied to the Allies. It was a significant strategic error, denying the Allies the opportunity greatly to shorten their lines of communication and to deliver the logistic resources necessary to allow their fighting elements to pursue the Germans.

Field Marshal Montgomery, commanding the British 21st Army Group, believed strongly that the key to success was for a thrust involving forty-two divisions to drive through the Ruhr and head for Berlin. To be successful it would require the dedication of almost all the logistic support available to the Allied Armies in Europe, and would bring those not involved in the thrust, principally the Americans to his south, to a virtual standstill. This was the infamous 'broad front against narrow' argument that raged among the various senior Allied commanders. Broad over narrow was something of an exaggeration, as Montgomery was wont to point out after the war. A force of forty-two divisions was, in his view, hardly a needle-like thrust. Montgomery viewed it as the 'knock-out blow' that was required to beat the Germans once and for all and to bring the war to a speedy close. This was especially important to a nation, the United Kingdom, which was rapidly approaching the stage where it would be demographically incapable of prosecuting the war at the same level of intensity given that it was also having to support a number of other theatres, principally the Far East.

Eisenhower did not agree with Montgomery's idea and resolved to stick to his broad front approach, employing all his armies at the same time. He was concerned that the offensive might run out of steam with the length of the logistic tail, and be heavily counter-attacked; an undertaking at which the Germans were past-masters. Were that to happen he would have nothing in reserve to mount a rescue or to reinforce. Furthermore, logistic shortages elsewhere would render the rest of his forces unable to fight, and therefore prone to German counter-attacks and outflanking movements.

However, by the end of the first week in September 1944 things were happening that caused Eisenhower to adjust his position. Already deeply concerned by the impact of logistic shortages on his overall advance and under pressure from Montgomery, he also had, sitting in the UK, 1st Allied Airborne Army. It was a highly trained, very expensive asset, and it was doing nothing. He was under considerable

Lieutenant General Frederick 'Boy' Browning.

political and military pressure to make use of it. It was, in a sense, an Army looking for a role, but could only be of use provided a worthwhile operation could be found for it. What finally tipped the balance, however, was that on 8 September V2 rockets, very much more potent than their V1 predecessors, began to land on London from launch sites in Holland. The impact was not just to inflict fear on the civilian population, it was also placing the future of Churchill's government at risk. Therefore, when Eisenhower met Montgomery at Brussels airport on 10 September 1944 and was shown the concept for the use of a corps of airborne soldiers in the Netherlands, he was readily persuaded that it was a risk worth taking.

The plan was that 1st Airborne Corps, commanded by Lieutenant General Frederick 'Boy' Browning and comprising three airborne divisions, would drop along the main highway leading from the Belgian border into Holland to the Dutch town of Arnhem on the lower Rhine, through Eindhoven and Nijmegen. They were to lay a 'carpet' of airborne troops, taking all the bridges along the route, over which the British XXX Corps would roll. Once taken, with the 'corridor' secure, the crossing over the Rhine at Arnhem would allow the British to break out into the North German Plain; to isolate Germany's industrial heartland in the Ruhr; to take Antwerp from the north; and to reach the V2 launch sites on the Dutch coast.

However, because of the distance and the numbers of troops available, there would be quite significant gaps between each of the airborne divisions through and across which the enemy could roam. It was much less a carpet and more a series of rugs. The US 101st Airborne Division would take the bridges north of Eindhoven, the US 82nd Airborne Division those in the Nijmegen area and the 1st British Airborne Division, reinforced by the 1st Independent Polish Parachute Brigade, was to take and hold the road bridge over the Lower Rhine at Arnhem. The operation was code-named MARKET GARDEN: MARKET for the airborne element and GARDEN for the ground forces.

The plan called for the first landings to take place on Sunday 17 September 1944, just seven days after Eisenhower had given his assent. This was the third Sunday in the month, the day on which Battle of Britain Sunday is now commemorated annually. On the same day the ground forces would commence their move up the single narrow road that was the sixty-five mile corridor to Arnhem. Montgomery's promise to Browning was that he would be in Arnhem in two days to relieve the paratroopers. Browning expressed the view that they could

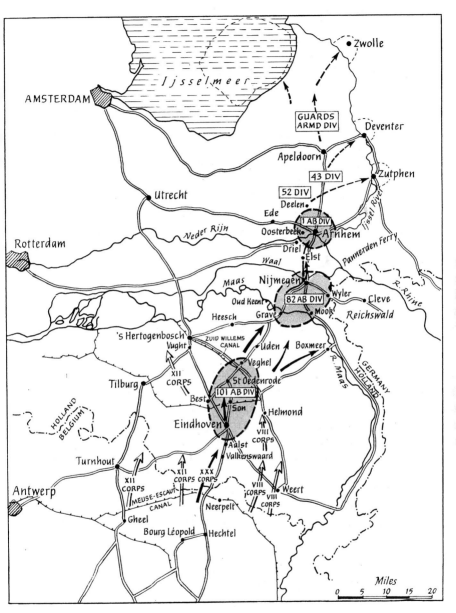

Operation Market Garden: The Plan.

hold for four, and it was at this stage he is said to have made his remark about it being possibly a bridge too far.

The reality is that any forces crossing the River Waal at Nijmegen are encased between the sea to the west, the Waal running through Nijmegen and the lower Rhine in Arnhem. They are on an island, called in Dutch The Bettuwe, and the only way off the island is to cross the Arnhem Bridge or retrace one's steps back south of Nijmegen. Strategically, therefore, it was two bridges too far. It is unclear if Browning ever used the words attributed to him, but if he did his paratroopers kept their word – and held his Bridge for almost four days. It was not their fault that it turned out to be one bridge too many.

1st Airborne Division

Commanded by Major General Roy Urquhart, the Division comprised three brigades each of three battalions, supported from within the division by some specialist troops: artillery, engineers, communications, medical and logistic units. These are known under the collective title of divisional troops. Two of the brigades were parachute brigades, although they each had an element, almost entirely where vehicles or heavier equipment such as artillery, were taken into battle by glider. The other brigade was airlanded, transported to battle entirely by glider. For divisional troops, including logistic and support elements, the majority were gliderborne, with just a few parachuting in.

For each of the brigades and divisional troops, a large slice of the logistic support came overland. These units, collectively called the Seaborne Echelon, had to take their place on the corridor leading to Arnhem from the Belgian border. They only managed to reach as far as Nijmegen; just in time to help their comrades who were by then, withdrawing south across the Rhine. Until the seaborne logistic support caught up with them, the paratroopers would have to survive with the two days of supplies they took in with them by air, supplemented by aerially delivered stocks courtesy of the Royal Air Force.

There were significant differences between the structures of the infantry battalions in the parachute and airlanded brigades. Each parachute battalion comprised three rifle companies, each of three platoons. Their integral support weapons were limited to a platoon of six 3"-mortars and a platoon of eight Vickers .303" belt-fed machine-guns. Their only anti-tank capability lay with the PIAT, a weapon with a range of significantly less than 100 metres and with limited capability to damage a tank. Parachute battalions relied for their heavier anti-tank capability on a Royal Artillery anti-tank troop being attached to

1ST AIRBORNE DIVISION

HQ 1ST AIRBORNE DIVISION

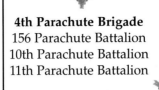

1st Airlanding Brigade

1st Battalion
The Border
Regiment

2nd Battalion
The South
Staffordshire
Regiment

7th Battalion
The King's Own
Scottish Borderers

1st Parachute Brigade
1st Parachute Battalion
2nd Parachute Battalion
3rd Parachute Battalion

4th Parachute Brigade
156 Parachute Battalion
10th Parachute Battalion
11th Parachute Battalion

1st Airborne
Reconnaissance
Squadron

DIVISIONAL TROOPS
21st Independent
Parachute Company

Royal Artillery
1st Airlanding Light Regiment
1st Airlanding Anti-Tank Battery
2nd Airlanding Anti-Tank Battery

Royal Engineers
1st Parachute Squadron
4th Parachute Squadron
9th Field Company Airborne
261 Field Park Company Airborne

Royal Signals
1st Company
2nd Company

Royal Army Medical Corps
16 Parachute Field Ambulance
133 Parachute Field Ambulance
181 Airlanding Field Ambulance

Royal Army Service Corps
93 Airborne Composite Company
250 Airborne Light Company
153 Airborne Composite Company

Royal Army Ordnance Corps
1st Airborne Division Ordnance
Field Park

Royal Electrical and Mechanical
Engineers
1st Airborne Division Workshop

Royal Military Police
1st Airborne Division Provost
Company

PIAT (Projector Infantry Anti-Tank).

Two British Infantrymen prepare to fire the PIAT.

them. These small sub-units brought with them six 6-pounder guns. The guns used solid shot to destroy tanks by punching a hole in them, but there was also a high explosive round available, giving them additional capability against personnel and buildings. It is unclear if this latter nature of ammunition formed part of the gun load at Arnhem.

It is worth noting that there was additional anti-tank capability at Arnhem, with the presence in each of the two Airlanding Anti-Tank

A 17-pounder anti-tank gun exhibited beside the Hartenstein museum.

Vickers medium machine gun.

batteries of two troops of four 17-pounder guns. Flown in complete with their Morris Convertible towing vehicle as a single load in a Hamilcar Glider, their presence came as a great shock to the Germans who had no idea that the British had the capability to transport them by air. They were very much more potent than the smaller 6-pounder and tended to be held in reserve above battalion level.

Airlanded battalions had four rifle companies, each with four platoons. The platoons were smaller than those in a parachute battalion, twenty-six strong so that each platoon comprised a Horsa glider load. For support weapons integral to the battalion they had a very powerful package. In the battalion support group there were two platoons each of 3"-mortars, Vickers machine-guns and 6-pounder anti-tank guns, a total of twelve mortar tubes, sixteen machine-guns and eight anti-tank guns, the latter being in addition to the PIATs carried throughout the rifle platoons. Parachute battalions deployed to Arnhem with some 550 men, airlanded battalions approximately 750.

Urquhart's Plan for the Assault

Major General Urquhart was forced into a three-phase assault on his key objective from landing and dropping zones that were some eight miles from the Arnhem Bridge. The three phases were because there were insufficient aircraft to lift the entire force of two American divisions and one British airborne division, and it would have to be done in three waves; one per day over three days. The distance from the objective was the result of Air Force insistence that dropping any closer would hazard too many aircraft from anti-aircraft batteries on and around the bridge itself, and at Deelen airfield to the north of the town and over which aircraft would have to fly if they dropped their loads at or near the bridge.

All sorties were to be in daylight. This was partly due to the lack of time properly to train transport aircraft crews, particularly American crews, in night formation flying on that scale. There were, however, other reasons: pin-pointing dropping and landing zones would be easier, the very real menace of German night fighters would be eliminated and since the anti-aircraft guns were controlled by radar they were as effective by night as by day – so ran the logic.

The pathfinders preceded the main drop, with 21st Independent Parachute Company dropping some thirty minutes ahead of the main body in order to mark out the DZs and LZs. Then, in his first wave, Urquhart went in with the forward elements of his divisional headquarters, together with 1st Parachute Brigade that was to make its

Major General Roy Urquhart standing in the grounds of the Hartenstein hotel.

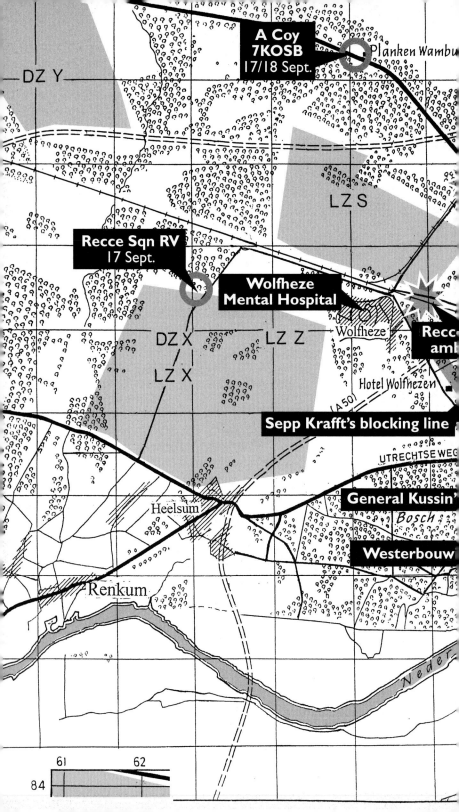

A Coy 7KOSB 17/18 Sept.

Planken Wambu

DZ Y

LZ S

Recce Sqn RV 17 Sept.

Wolfheze Mental Hospital

DZ X   LZ Z

Recce amb

LZ X

Wolfheze

Hotel Wolfhezen

Sepp Krafft's blocking line

UTRECHTSE WEG

General Kussin'

Bosch

Westerbouw

Heelsum

Renkum

Neder

61   62

84

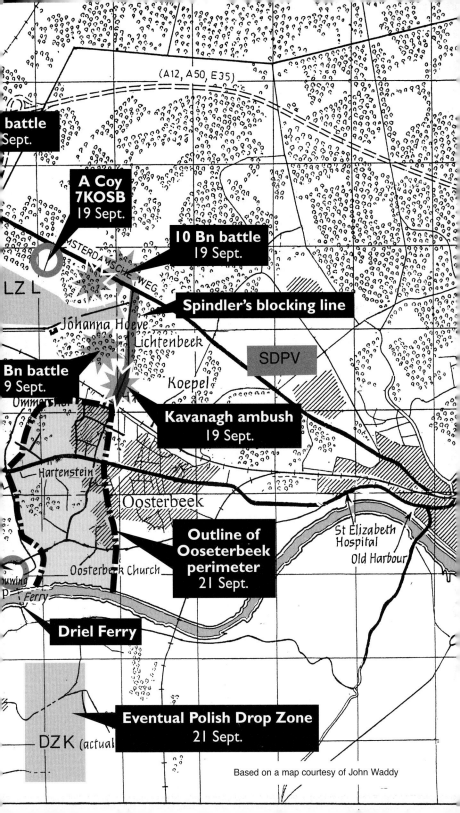

battle
Sept.

**A Coy
7KOSB**
19 Sept.

10 Bn battle
19 Sept.

(A12, A50, E35)

LZ L

AMSTERDAMSCHE WEG

Spindler's blocking line

Johanna Hoeve

Lichtenbeek

SDPV

**Bn battle
9 Sept.**

Koepel

Ommershof

Kavanagh ambush
19 Sept.

Hartenstein

Oosterbeek

**Outline of
Ooseterbeek
perimeter
21 Sept.**

St Elizabeth
Hospital
Old Harbour

Oosterbeek Church

uwing
p Ferry

Driel Ferry

Eventual Polish Drop Zone
21 Sept.

DZ K (actual

Based on a map courtesy of John Waddy

way to the bridge and secure it. On its way the brigade was also to secure a railway bridge and a pontoon bridge, both spanning the river to the west of the main road bridge. He was made aware of a ferry operating across the Lower Rhine at Heavadorp near a hill feature called the Westerbouwing, but ignored it as it was not included in his orders.

Also included in the first wave was the 1st Airlanding Brigade. Its task was to guard the dropping and landing zones for the second phase that would land the next day. This would be the whole of 4th Parachute Brigade, together with more divisional troops and artillery.

On the third day the last wave would be 1st Independent Polish Parachute Brigade, with their heavy equipment landing north of the river and the rest of the brigade parachuting in near the southern end of the main road bridge. This meant his division would not be complete until two days after the initial landings. This, coupled with the distance he had to cover to reach the bridge, eliminated any chance of him gaining the upper hand from the greatest attribute possessed by airborne troops: the ability to achieve total surprise.

The Brigades' Objectives

1st Airlanding Brigade would be the first to land, bringing its three battalions into LZ 'S'. Gliderborne troops were able to concentrate very much more quickly than their parachuting colleagues who tended to disperse after they had exited the aircraft. They would, therefore, be able to move swiftly to their allotted tasks defending the three areas on which the division was due to arrive over the next two days. The 2nd Battalion the South Staffordshire Regiment (2 South Staffords) was to remain on LZ 'S' to secure it in anticipation of the balance of the Airlanding Brigade arriving the next day. The principal element of this second lift would be the two companies the South Staffords had left behind due to a shortage of towing aircraft for the thirty-five gliders required to carry two companies of infantry. It is perhaps a coincidence that thirty-five towing aircraft were what was required to bring in Browning's Corps HQ in the 82nd Airborne Division area on that first day. With no communications, a half-formed HQ and no mobility it remains to this day hard to see what he felt he might have achieved on the ground in Holland that he could not have achieved very much more effectively by remaining in the United Kingdom. At least he would then have seen where he would be best placed and could have deployed accordingly, but as it was he had three divisions with which he virtually had no contact each fighting separate battles along a road occupied by elements of an Army Group with which he had no clear command relationship.

The 7th Battalion the King's Own Scottish Borderers (7 KOSB) was to move off north-west to secure the landing zone at South Ginkel Heath for the 4th Brigade drop the next day. Subsequently, their task would be to move, for the third day, to secure the LZ for the Polish heavy equipment due to arrive in gliders on LZ 'L'. The 1st Battalion the Border Regiment (1 Border) had the task of defending what was on D-Day DZ 'X', but which on D+1, 18 September 1944, would become LZ 'X' and on which 4th Brigade's gliders were to land. Once all these tasks were complete the brigade was to move to its position defending the western edge of the perimeter which Urquhart planned to throw around the Arnhem Bridge.

1st Parachute Brigade, comprising 1st, 2nd and 3rd Parachute Battalions, was to move directly from the DZs into the town. Conscious of the limitations imposed by the speed at which his marching infantry could cover the ground, especially with the heavy loads they carried, Urquhart chose to use his reconnaissance squadron, commanded by Major Freddie Gough, to rush as swiftly as it could to seize both ends of the bridge in a coup de main operation, and then to await the arrival of the infantry. This would involve the use of three of the squadron's four troops, each troop comprising three sections of two jeeps, each of which was fitted with a Vickers K machine gun and crewed by five men of the Reconnaissance Corps. It was a task to which the Reconnaissance Squadron was ill-suited. Its role, training and equipment were tailored to a reconnaissance role, and not to defensive or offensive operations against opposition of any significance.

In planning his route into the town Brigadier Gerald Lathbury, commanding 1st Parachute Brigade, chose to send his three infantry battalions along separate routes. He reasoned that they would arrive in force more quickly than if they formed a single column strung out for miles across the Dutch countryside. In so doing he was sacrificing control in order to gain speed and hence time to concentrate his force quicker on the objective. The risk was that in the event of serious opposition he would not be able to concentrate sufficiently quickly in order to overcome it. However, given the intelligence

Lieutenant Colonel J D Frost.

picture he rightly considered it a risk worth taking.

The 2nd Parachute Battalion commanded by Lieutenant Colonel J D Frost was to take the most southerly route, along a minor road running close to the Rhine. With it, in the same column, were Lathbury's brigade headquarters with its signallers and clerks; 9 Field Company Royal Engineers (RE); 16 Field Ambulance Royal Army Medical Corps (RAMC), which was to drop off at the St Elizabeth Hospital a mile or so west of the bridge; the 3rd Parachute Platoon RASC, from 250 Airborne Light Company RASC, carrying the brigade's reserve of two days' ammunition; and a party of an officer and five soldiers of the Royal Army Ordnance Corps (RAOC) from the divisional Ordnance Field Park who were to secure storage sites by the bridge. In addition to securing the main Arnhem Bridge, Frost was tasked with capturing the railway bridge and pontoon bridge across the Rhine en route to his main objective.

Lieutenant Colonel J A C Fitch's 3rd Parachute Battalion was to follow the middle route, passing through the centre of Oosterbeek to go direct to the bridge with no intermediate objectives. On the northern route, Lieutenant Colonel D T Dobie's 1st Battalion was to move to secure an area of the town to the north of the bridge to protect against potential incursion from the north.

Feldmarschall Model. Were the British paratroopers assigned to capture or kill him? At first he seriously considered that possibility.

On the second day, Brigadier J W Hackett's 4th Parachute Brigade was to secure the area to the north of the bridge, having moved along the line of the Ede-Arnhem road from its dropping zone on the South Ginkel Heath – the furthest dropping zone of them all from the objective. On the third day the Poles would land on the polder just south of the bridge to secure the eastern edge of the divisional perimeter, with 1st Parachute Brigade responsible for the southern part. The Polish heavy equipment was to be brought in by glider to LZ 'L' on the same day.

The Germans

Arnhem was very much a rear area in the German deployment in that part of Europe. The units were involved in training and low-level garrison duties; some were Dutch SS.

However, shortly before the airborne landings *Feldmarschall* Model had ordered II SS Panzer Corps into the area north-east of Arnhem to rest and refit. Comprising the 9th SS (*Hohenstaufen*) and 10th SS (*Frundsberg*) Divisions, it was a force that had been gravely battered in the fighting in France in July and August 1944. However, despite limitations in equipment and in manpower it was a potent threat, with advantages of firepower, locally available logistic support and communications that the lightly equipped paratroopers who were to land at Oosterbeek to assault the Arnhem Bridge simply did not possess.

There were a number of key factors which impacted upon the German reaction to the airborne landings, and which were to have such a profound effect on Urquhart and his men. However, one rumour can easily be dispelled: there is no evidence whatsoever that the Germans were expecting the attack. There is no suggestion that they possessed prior intelligence, either from their own sources or provided by disaffected pro-German Dutch. They were taken completely by surprise.

Three important points favoured the Germans:

Firstly, the presence of *Feldmarschall* Model in Oosterbeek as the landings took place. One of Germany's most able Army commanders, he was perfectly placed to coordinate German defensive activity, which included operations against the Americans in Nijmegen as well as the British in Arnhem and Oosterbeek.

Secondly, SS-*Gruppenführer* Wilhelm Bittrich and the two divisions (9th SS (*Hohenstaufen*) and 10th SS (*Frundsberg*)) of his II Panzer SS Corps just to the north-east of Arnhem, placed there in order to refit.

Thirdly, SS-*Sturmbahnführer* Sepp Krafft and his SS Training Battalion operating in the woods around Wolfheze, just to the east of the British

**SS-Gruppenführer
Wilhelm Bittrich**

dropping and landing zones. They would be on hand to respond swiftly to the early landings, and having trained earlier that year in countering landings by airborne troops they knew precisely what to do. Relatively small in number the Battalion's actions were to have a disproportionate effect on 1st British Airborne Division.

The refitting of Bittrich's Corps was important for it would become a major asset in von Rundstedt's armoury as he attempted to stem the invasion of Germany from the west by the Allies. A great deal of early work was already underway and officers and soldiers alike were striving to ensure that the work was undertaken swiftly. They were also determined to have available as much equipment as they could when the time came, once more, to fight. Consequently, when the 9th SS were ordered to hand all their fit equipment to the 10th prior to proceeding back to Germany to refit with new vehicles and weapons a number, commanders and soldiers alike, were reticent. They were delighted to be going back to Germany, for whatever reason, but were not prepared to be left, even for a very short while, without the means to fight given that the situation could change very suddenly. Therefore, a significant amount of the 9th's stock of vehicles and heavy weapons were deliberately disabled so that they would not need to be handed over to the 10th SS, but were capable of regeneration within a few hours should the need arise.

Whilst II Panzer SS Corps was a potent weapon in the battle against the airborne soldiers at Arnhem and Oosterbeek, there were other German formations and units elsewhere in the Netherlands whose presence was also to have a profound effect on the eventual fate of the paratroopers who landed north of the Rhine.

Further south, on the Dutch/Belgian Border, *Generaloberst* Kurt Student was assembling a force known as 1st Parachute Army. It was an Army in name only, but it was stiffened with some first class fighting material drawn in from Germany. Student's orders were to build a new front on the Albert Canal, and then to hold it at all costs. The German capacity for organisation and improvisation, especially under extreme pressure, was considerable and some of the units were actually in position and being equipped on the spot within 24 hours of Student receiving his orders on 4 September 1944 – the day Antwerp fell. Of the rest of his units, some comprised soldiers with disabilities and illnesses, but inadequate as they might have seemed this really was a case of all hands to the pump in order to keep the Allies from reaching and then crossing the German border. There were also some elements of experienced fighting formations joining in. And 'joining in' summed up the situation in many cases. For example, *Generalleutnant* Kurt Chill's 85th Division had suffered heavy losses in France. On his move north away from the fighting and under orders to proceed to Germany he had picked up stragglers from other units. However, on his way to Germany he heard of the fall of Brussels and decided to stay. With the battlegroup he was able to form he was instrumental in repelling the first British attempts to cross the Meuse-Escaut Canal on the Dutch-Belgian border.

Also in the south, and actually south of Antwerp, was General von Zangen's 15th Army, held against the coast by the advancing Allied armies. He was ordered to evacuate it across the River Scheldt and into the south of the Netherlands. In sixteen days he successfully moved the remnants of nine battered infantry divisions, completing the task on 21 September 1944. Two of these divisions

Generaloberst Kurt Student.

became available to hold the line to the right of Student's 1st Parachute Army, thereby completing a shaky, but gradually strengthening, barrier through which XXX Corps was going to have to break. They were plugging a gap which just a fortnight earlier had been there to drive through unopposed if only the Allies had possessed the wherewithal. These two formations would slow XXX Corps' advance and impose part of the delay that would lead to their late arrival north of Nijmegen on the approaches to Arnhem.

Further north, with their demarcation line on the Rivers Maas and Waal, were the soldiers of Armed Forces Command in the Netherlands. Some were in a collection of formed units, some had a role in manning and looking after installations in what was the German rear area. Others were *ad hoc* groupings of men from those retreating from the fighting in France and Belgium. Others were training units and yet more were created from *Luftwaffe* personnel. *Generalleutnant* Hans von Tettau commanded just such a collection of units operating a screen on the River Waal. He also controlled the SS Panzer-Grenadier Depot and Reserve Battalion 16, already mentioned as being commanded by SS-

Sturmbahnführer Sepp Krafft and located in Oosterbeek.

Somehow, this disparate collection of men, units and formations were going to have to work against the combined efforts of a 21st Army Group advance, spearheaded by XXX Corps and with its way paved by an airborne corps in what was to be the largest airborne operation ever undertaken, before or since. That they were able to do so effectively remains a testament to the professionalism and ability of German soldiers and officers, both on the staff and in command, and especially to the junior leaders in direct contact with the Allies.

Our story begins in Oosterbeek, from just beside the former HQ of 1st British Airborne Division at the Hartenstein Hotel; now the Airborne Museum 'Hartenstein'.

The Hartenstein Hotel, Headquarters of the 1st British Airborne Division, taken after the batlle. Courtesy Drs Robert P G A Voskuil.

CHAPTER TWO

THE LANDINGS AND THE FIRST MOVES

Duration – Two and a half hours by car
Distance – 20 miles or 32 Kilometres

Starting from the Airborne Museum 'Hartenstein': Set the trip meter to zero and from the car park behind the Kleyn Hartensteyn Restaurant, move to Utrechtseweg to **turn left** to follow the main road. As you do so begin to think of distances – long and short – since distance is something that will come to dominate your appreciation of what happened. As you make the left turn onto Utrechtseweg you will glance to your right to check traffic and will see the Oosterbeek Crossroads at the traffic lights about 100 metres away. This crossroads marks the eastern boundary of what would eventually be the Oosterbeek perimeter.

Drive along Utrechtseweg past the Hartenstein Hotel on the left and the monument on the right, and with your trip meter reading **0.6 miles/1 km** reach a roundabout that marks what was known in 1944 as the Koude Herberg (Cold Inn) crossroads, now Oude Herberg (Old Inn). As you go **straight over** following Utrechtseweg glance to the left down the road heading downhill from the roundabout and this is part of the western boundary of the Oosterbeek perimeter. Bearing in mind the short distance you have travelled you will be beginning to get a feel for how small was the area into which 1st Airborne Division was crammed following its failure to reach, in full strength, the Bridge at Arnhem.

Utrechtseweg is the middle route of the three taken by 1st Parachute Brigade in its attempt to reach the Bridge, and was used by 3rd Parachute Battalion.

The Koude (Oude) Herberg crossroads looking west, replaced in 1999 with a roundabout. Courtesy Drs Robert P G A Voskuil.

You are driving in the opposite direction to that taken by the paratroopers, and by the end of this tour will have returned to the area just beyond the roundabout to see what happened to them. In the meantime, you should follow the road, noting as you do the well-kept gardens with their fences and hedges very similar to the way they appeared in 1944. These fences and hedges were to prove a real nuisance, making it very difficult for soldiers, friend and foe alike, to move easily, especially when under fire. It is something worth keeping in your mind throughout your tour of the area.

The trip meter registers **2.6 miles/4.2 kms** at a crossroads with traffic lights. **Turn right**, still on Utrechtseweg and **signed Renkum**, follow the road under the bridge and **turn right** shortly after it up Bennekomseweg. The road bears left after 100 metres and then almost immediately on the left is a small memorial beside a lay-by in which it is possible to **park.**

The Heelsum Memorial: 6-pounder anti-tank gun and parachute re-supply containers. Courtesy Drs Robert P G A Voskuil.

The memorial comprises a 6-pounder anti tank gun, beneath an arch constructed of containers used to deliver stores by air. These containers were the type dropped from the bomb bays of Stirlings over Oosterbeek. They would normally contain weapons, food, ammunition and radios. The other containers used in air dropping stores, a process known as 'air despatch', were wicker baskets, examples of which can

38

be seen in the Hartenstein Museum. They were either ejected from the bomb bays of the Stirlings, four per sortie, or from the side door at the rear of a Dakota's fuselage, sixteen per sortie.

There were fifty-two 6-pounder anti-tank guns despatched with the British to Arnhem, twenty-four with the three infantry battalions in the Airlanding Brigade and the balance with the two Royal Artillery anti-tank batteries. The Polish Brigade also sent some in, but they were almost completely destroyed on landing and played virtually no part in the battle. With a calibre of 57mm and an effective range of 500 metres it was a powerful weapon for its size. It defeated enemy armour using armour-piercing shot. Literally punching a hole through protective plating it would go through 146mm of armour.

Drive on up Bennekomseweg taking care to **keep to the right** until you reach a roundabout at **4.1 miles/6.6 km**. **Turn right** along Telefoonweg and you will see in front of you DZ 'X' and LZ 'Z' on the wide expanse of arable land to your left and right, bordered by pine forests in the middle distance. Telefoonweg was the road used by the pilots of the aircraft and the gliders as their visual marker for the Landing and Dropping Zones for the first day. **Do not stop** or get out at this stage as the narrow road does not lend itself to this; and there will be an opportunity to do so in a few minutes. As you drive slowly along this road imagine that in 1944 the gliders of the Divisional HQ, Divisional Troops and those belonging to the battalions of 1st Parachute Brigade would have been on your right whilst the Brigade's parachutists would have been mainly on your left, with some dropping to your right near the road.

At the top of the DZ/LZ is a small car park on the left in the corner of a wood, trip meter reading **5.6 miles/9 kilometres**. **Park here**, leave the car and look out along Telefoonweg to the south across Dropping Zone 'X' and Landing Zone 'Z'. Immediately behind you, to the north and about 400 metres away through the trees, is Landing Zone 'S', the destination of the Airlanding Brigade; and you will see that shortly.

On 17 September 1944 at 12.30 pm twelve Stirling bombers appeared from the south through the slight haze of a sunny day flying directly towards the spot on which you are standing. They had taken off from RAF Fairford in Gloucestershire at 10.00 am and they contained the six officers and 180 men of 21st Independent Parachute Company, packed in at around sixteen men per aircraft.

The Parachute Regiment

These were the pathfinders. Trained to an exacting standard their role was to mark out the DZs and LZs for the main force, which was about half an hour behind.

Flying at just 600 feet the first six aircraft would have flown directly over your head, carrying the Company Headquarters and one platoon onto LZ 'S'. The other six deposited their loads, one platoon, each of some 48 men, onto the centre of DZ 'X' and LZ 'Z', before joining up once more as a group of twelve and heading back home. Floating silently down into occupied Holland, and not quite knowing what to expect, the pathfinder paratroopers went swiftly and methodically about their business. Some took up protective defensive positions whilst others busied themselves setting up Eureka Beacons onto which aircraft could home and yet more set up white panels and positioned smoke markers to await the arrival of the main body. The DZ for 1st Parachute Brigade was marked with its identifying letter, 'X', in large white panels, together with a 'T' shaped symbol, with the stem of the letter pointing in the direction of the wind. The LZs for the gliders had only the identifying letter.

By 1.00 pm they had done their job. All the markers were in place and everything was set. There had been a couple of skirmishes with some Germans with a few prisoners taken, but there was no enemy activity to speak of. Given where they were and what they had achieved it was remarkably peaceful. They settled down to wait, and then they heard in the distance the sound of the engines. Muted at first, it grew in strength as the huge numbers of aircraft bringing in two airborne brigades and their divisional headquarters approached. All hell was about to be let loose in this quiet corner of this most peaceful but occupied country; and no one, not least the Germans, had any idea what was coming.

The first to arrive were the gliders. Passing to the half-left of where you are standing and about fifteen hundred metres away the first to appear were the 134 gliders of the Airlanding Brigade that had made it this far, targeted to land on LZ 'S', beyond the trees behind where you are standing, of which more later. After some twenty minutes more gliders carrying divisional HQ and divisional troops arrived, to land to your half-left in the open ground on the left of Telefoonweg. They had been released by their towing aircraft at about two miles range to the LZ and at a height of between 3,000 and 4,000 feet. As they levelled out to land the pilots were denied the usual ninety-degree turn favoured for gliders in order to slow down, get their bearings and make a well-ordered landing. They were coming in straight from the flight path,

The RAF's Short Stirling. TAYLOR LIBRARY

and because of this there was a tendency to come in too fast and overshoot the prescribed landing spot. With the first gliders landing at the north end of the LZ, and subsequent aircraft landing progressively further and further south, some of those first landings overshot and ended up in the trees bordering the road at the northern end.

Looking south from the car park in the direction from which the gliders and aircraft approached. Telefoonweg is on the left.

A Hamilcar Glider. Courtesy Museum of Army Flying

A Horsa Glider. TAYLOR LIBRARY

A Jeep being loaded onto a Horsa Glider on an exercise. TAYLOR LIBRARY

There were two glider types used at Arnhem: the Horsa and the Hamilcar. The Horsa was the smaller of the two, and by far the great majority, able to carry twenty-six fully equipped troops together with a handcart in which they placed additional ammunition and stores. It could also carry, for example, a jeep towing two trailers together with the jeep crew, or one of the 75mm howitzers of the 1st Airlanding Light Regiment.

The Hamilcar was very much larger, and their role at Arnhem was, principally, to fly in Bren carriers, of which for example, there were two per parachute battalion, and the 17-pounder anti-tank guns in the two Airlanding Anti-Tank Batteries. Three Hamilcars were also used, on the second day, for the carriage of a bulk reserve of stores and equipment.

The landing was hard for the large Hamilcars, as they had no nose wheel. When the two landing wheels, located on either side of the fuselage under the wings, sank into soft ground the aircraft would often pivot forward, the nose would dip, the tail was forced up and, in a two cases, the glider was forced over in an ungainly forward roll onto its back. Many of the passengers were badly hurt in these crashes – often with serious crush injuries. The pilots, with the cockpit on top of the aircraft, were particularly vulnerable; and some were killed. Sergeant N G 'Bill' Griffin of Divisional HQ saw one such incident.

'Hamilcars had a problem landing. I saw a man screaming from his injuries following a bad landing. I gave him morphine and left him. It was all I could do for him.'

Bill Griffin had been in the second glider to leave Fairford, and he did not enjoy the ride. Part of the reason lay with the flak his glider encountered crossing Holland. As if that were not enough, just as they were coming in to land another glider went straight past their front. Bill's glider, in which there was a jeep and trailer in addition to its passengers, veered and they landed hard on the nose. The pilot was all right, but the tail was in the air and the load rendered useless.

However, most of the landings were successful, and very quickly the LZ was full of men departing from the side door of the aircraft to go to their rendezvous, marked by coloured smoke. Others were undoing the three retaining bolts on each side to release the Horsa tail section and remove it to allow vehicles or 6-pounder guns to exit and be moved away to join their units. The nose sections of Hamilcars were being elevated so that guns and carriers could depart and go about their business.

As they did so in the comparative silence of a glider landing and its aftermath the noise from the south heralded the arrival of yet more

A Dakota. Courtesy Museum of Army Flying.

Horsa gliders on the Landing Zone with their fuselages opened up.

units. The aircraft, Dakotas of the United States' 314th Troop Carrier Group, would drop paratroopers onto the open ground of DZ 'X', immediately in front of where you are standing. This time, however, the sequence was reversed. The first aircraft to arrive ejected their paratroopers at the southern end of the DZ, furthest away from where you are standing, and then progressively further north. There were nineteen men per aircraft, with the 'planes operating in groups of nine across the area. The pilots would throttle back to adopt a speed as close to stalling as they safely could, and the first parachutist jumped at 600 feet.

The soldiers were wearing the normal webbing for an infantry soldier, and had strapped to their leg a kit bag containing those items they could not sensibly carry on their backs whilst parachuting. This included their personal weapon and any additional equipment they might have to carry, such as, perhaps, a radio or a PIAT. Having jumped they first checked that the parachute was functioning. They then turned their attention to the kit bag. It had to be released from the leg and then lowered on a rope attached to their waist to the point where it dangled some fifteen feet below them. A kit bag was supposed to carry up to eighty pounds in weight, but they were frequently overloaded. To land with the bag still attached to the leg guaranteed a broken limb, so lowering it properly was an important procedure, and it had all to be completed within the fifteen or so seconds between leaving the aircraft and hitting the ground.

Because of its slow speed and the need to maintain a level flight posture the aircraft lost height during the run over the DZ. Consequently, when the last of the nineteen men in a stick jumped he did so from a lower height than the first; sometimes as much as 100 feet lower. These men had to work very hard to sort out their airborne administration in the time left before they landed.

It could be a confusing experience, with a great deal to do in a very short time. Private Ted Mordecai's abiding memory was: 'the despatcher's "best of luck, cheerio". He was all right, he'd be back home for tea.' He and his friend Kevin Heaney, both RAOC soldiers, were to rendezvous with 2nd Parachute Battalion before heading for the Arnhem Bridge. Kevin's jump, however, was not without its problems.

The Royal Army Ordnance Crops.

'As my parachute opened my helmet fell off and it landed before me. I thought: 'this is a good start.' However, when I landed the

Ted Mordecai and Kevin Heaney board a Dakota at Barkestone Heath. Imperial War Museum

helmet, slightly dented, was only about ten yards away and, after taking off my harness, I picked it up and was able to wear it quite satisfactorily. We then made our way quickly to the rendezvous point. There did not appear to be any urgency; the sun was warm, everything was peaceful – had we really dropped into enemy territory?'

The Border Regiment.

Captain Ingram Cleasby of 1 Border, who had landed by glider nearly an hour before the parachute drop, remembers clearly the sight and sound of 1st Parachute Brigade arriving.

'We had, thankfully, moved away from our gliders and we were taking up our pre-determined positions. Then we heard the roar of approaching aircraft coming in from the south-west. As wave after wave passed over us, the sky was filled with bursting parachutes. Moments later it was empty as the paratroopers reached the ground and almost immediately the great open polder was like a field of mushrooms with parachutes

scattered all over it. It was an amazing sight. And then within minutes local men and women came running across the near empty field, appearing from nowhere to greet us. Such high hopes soon to be disappointed.[1]

However, the event was not without its fatalities. There was probably only one malfunctioning parachute, or so the available reports would have it. Ted Mordecai, however, having landed safely, was subject to a rude shock:

'Overhead the Dakotas were still spilling out their contents and above them some Spitfires were circling the DZ. It was then I saw our first casualty. A chap was coming down with a kit bag dangling below him. I think it must have contained mortar bombs already fuzed up because as the bag hit the ground it exploded with a mighty bang. As he was only about twenty feet above it he caught the full blast and there wasn't much left of him.'

There were other reports of an explosion, said to be near the location of the Eureka Beacon[2], and initially 1 Platoon of the Pathfinder Company had believed themselves to be under attack. It seems that whatever happened one unfortunate soul died without even landing. However, there was no time to think about anything but getting on. Picking up their kit, assembling their weapons and looking about them to see what was what men moved off towards rendezvous points marked in smoke from canisters positioned by men of 21 Independent Parachute Company. The Brigade was getting ready to make its move.

Most of them would be departing from the south-east of the area towards the middle and lower routes. However, the car park in which you are standing continues to be important to our story, as does Telefoonweg. In 1944 the car park was just the corner of a wood, but it was the rendezvous for the Divisional Reconnaissance Squadron, manned by soldiers of the Reconnaissance Corps and commanded by Major Freddie Gough. They operated in sections of two vehicles with three sections to a troop. A junior officer commanded each section. If you allow your imagination to drift a little you can picture them all round you, with a growing sense of impatience as they awaited the order to move.

Reconnaissance Corps.

Their task was to rush ahead of the Brigade and take the Bridge early, to await the arrival of their slower moving infantry colleagues. However, there were unexplained delays and they left later than one might have expected. There was a story, quite untrue, that most of their vehicles failed to arrive and so they could not carry out their allotted task. In fact, only some of A Troop's vehicles did not make it, and as the Troop's task was locally in the area of the DZs and LZs it meant that almost all the vehicles allocated to the Bridge task were available.

We will now drive and follow the Reconnaissance Squadron route, but before doing so **walk to the edge of the car park and look to the left** along Telefoonweg.

This is the route that was followed by the Reconnaissance Squadron, and by 1st Parachute Battalion on its northern route to the area of the Bridge in Arnhem. Coming the other way, to take up their allotted positions in defence of DZ 'X' and LZ 'Z', would have been men of the Border Regiment, for the next day the balance of Divisional HQ gliders would come in on LZ 'Z', whilst DZ 'X' would become LZ 'X' ready to accept the gliderborne elements of the 4th Parachute Brigade. The parachutists of the 4th Brigade would land elsewhere, as we shall see.

Returning to your car, move **out of the car park and turn left** to continue along Telefoonweg, following the route taken by Freddie Gough's Divisional Reconnaissance Squadron. As you do so it is perhaps worth remembering that if you were to have turned right to follow the 2nd Parachute Battalion route to the Bridge in Arnhem from here by road it is exactly 8 miles or 12.8 kilometres.

After about 100 metres the **road bears sharp right**, and you should follow it. Just **as you make the turn** you will see facing you a track over the railway line. It is along this track that the men of 1 Border made their way to their positions from LZ 'S' which is through the trees to your front, to the north.

After the right turn, and at a safe and convenient place of your choosing, you might wish to stop.

Looking to your right you will see the vast expanse of LZ 'Z', and you will be parked in the very tree line into which something like nine gliders embedded themselves in overshooting the LZ. Shortly before you move off, glance to your left at the railway line, and, remembering where the Border Regiment crossed it, spare a thought for two young Cumbrian lads who formed a PIAT crew.

Lance Corporal 'Ginger' Wilson and Private Frank Aston of 11 Platoon, B Company were ordered to cover the railway line with the objective of firing at any locomotive that might appear from either west or east. Given the size of the potential target, and the limited

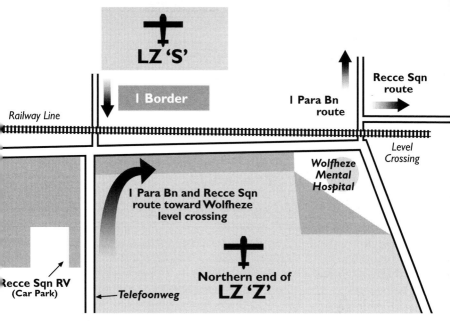

The Reconnaissance Squadron route.

capabilities and range of the PIAT, this was a task best described as 'different'. What Messrs Wilson and Aston thought of it is probably not printable; and would have been less so had they known there was a national rail strike and there were no trains running.

Let us now return to the Reconnaissance Squadron, and to 1st Parachute Battalion, whose route we are now following. Before driving off it is worth taking a moment to consider timings, which at this stage were crucial.

By 2.45 pm all the battalions had made their rendezvous and their radios were in communication with each other. At 3.00 pm the 2nd and 3rd Parachute Battalions moved off at the southern edge of the landing zones heading for the lower and middle routes. At about 3.20 pm Urquhart was given the erroneous message that most of the Reconnaissance Squadron transport had been lost and they would not be making the rush to the bridge as planned, and at 3.30 pm 1st Parachute Battalion was given the order to move.

It was not until 3.40 pm that the Reconnaissance Squadron began its move. There is no real explanation for the delay, except that it took some time to bring together all the vehicles that were to go to the bridge. They may also have been waiting for the four vehicles of 9 Field Company Royal Engineers that were to accompany them. However,

Johannahoeveweg as it becomes a dirt track.
Courtesy Drs Robert P A Voskuil.

these had landed by mistake on LZ 'S', not 'Z', and never joined the Squadron. Realising the importance of their mission, and chafing at the delay, Lieutenant Peter Bucknall commanding 8 Section of C Troop, on hearing the order to move, leapt to his vehicle, grabbed the first three men of his section he could and, ignoring the man-to-vehicle allocation that had been pre-planned before departure, drove helter-skelter out of the RV towards Arnhem. His vehicle would have driven past where you are now parked and according to reports he was driving very fast. His section sergeant, Tom McGregor, was left behind at the RV to gather the rest of Bucknall's men and follow him, which he did a few moments later.

Drive on until you reach the **level crossing turn left** and **immediately right** into Johannahoeveweg and **stop** as soon as you sensibly and safely can on the right

Reconnaissance Squadron tactics were such that vehicles moved as section groups of two, moving forward from position to position being covered by other vehicle sections who were stationary and on guard against potential enemy interference. It was a process known today as 'leapfrogging'. In front of Bucknall's two vehicles, therefore, were those of 7 and 9 Section, whilst C Troop HQ brought up the rear. At the Wolfheze railway station crossroads, 9 Section went over the railway

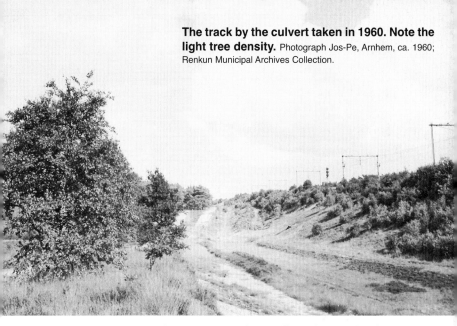

The track by the culvert taken in 1960. Note the light tree density. Photograph Jos-Pe, Arnhem, ca. 1960; Renkun Municipal Archives Collection.

line and took position at the entrance to the small road immediately right over the level crossing. Called Johannahoeveweg, it parallels the railway line. Just behind them, on the south side of the railway, near the entrance to the mental home, 7 Section positioned itself. Between them the two sections created a 'safe' gateway through which Bucknall would pass to lead the squadron along Johannahoeveweg.

Follow the route taken by 8 Section and Johannahoeveweg becomes a dirt track after about 100 metres going straight on at the junction with the turning into Mansveltweg on the left and with the trip meter reading **7.4 miles/11.8 km**. Going down the dirt track imagine yourself in the position of Sergeant McGregor with your section commander racing ahead out of sight, you are trying to catch up and suddenly there is the sound of firing ahead. Pressing on, McGregor was anxious to find out what was going on.

As you drive along the wooded track you will emerge into open ground with heath on the left, a post-war motorway bridge 100 metres ahead and a tunnel under the railway embankment to your right. **Pull over to the right and stop** just off the track in **front of the small tunnel**. It is just here, on the track, as it emerged into the open ground, that Sergeant McGregor's jeep was struck across the front by a burst of machine gun fire, probably from the high railway embankment up to the right.

Major Sepp Krafft, reacting instantly to the parachute drop, had moved his training battalion into a blocking position along

51

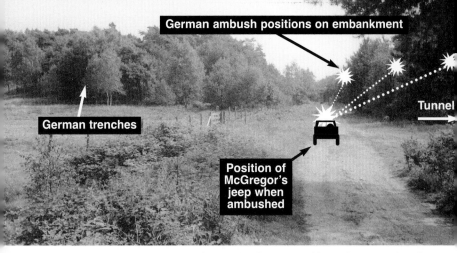

German ambush positions on embankment

German trenches

Tunnel

Position of McGregor's jeep when ambushed

Johannahoeveweg at the ambush scene. Note the tree density today. Sergeant McGregor's jeep was stopped on the track just by where the modern gate now stands on the left. The small track to the right reaches the tunnel under the railway in 20 metres.

Wolfhezerweg. Where you turned left over the railway just a few moments ago, the road to your right is part of Wolfhezerweg, and from where you stand now it is on the other side of the steep embankment and away to the south. However, concerned about his exposed right flank, and wishing to protect it, Krafft had put his reserve platoon on the north side of the embankment near where you are standing and across onto the small hill to the left of the track, just this side of the modern motorway bridge. In the time it took the paratroopers, and particularly the Reconnaissance Squadron, to get organised and move off Sepp Krafft had, unknowingly, straddled the Squadron's route.

The machine-gun fire wounded one man, Trooper Minns. Two of the others jumped from the jeep and with the wounded man crawled under the vehicle. The remaining three sought cover on the open ground to the left of the track, Sergeant McGregor in a shallow ditch and the others behind some small trees. The section's difficulty was that they could see clearly Germans moving about on the hill to the left of the track, but could see nothing on the embankment and it was from here that the fire was coming. In seeking to find out what was going on, Sergeant McGregor was killed. Trooper Arthur Barlow saw it happen:

> '*I remember seeing Sergeant McGregor rear himself up on his hands to have a look around. He fell flat on his face and died without making a sound.*[3]'

Within the next few minutes the four remaining soldiers were wounded by rifle and machine-gun fire from the German positions all around them. Exposed, as they were, their sergeant dead, no idea what had happened to their officer and all having been hit they had no choice but to surrender. The German sergeant who came down to take them prisoner spoke perfect English, and took the four less seriously wounded away. Minns was too seriously hurt to be moved and the German assured them someone would be back for him, although it never happened.

Further back up the track 7 Section had heard the firing, and dismounted to move forward on foot. Initially they saw the wounded men. However, the section moved back to report what had been seen and it was during that time that the injured soldiers had been taken prisoner. There followed a number of attempts by the Troop to recover Minns, during which one of the 9 Section men saw Bucknall's vehicle burning and with dead bodies around it in the area of the modern motorway bridge. There were further casualties in C Troop, two of which resulted in death. One of them, Trooper Edmond, was badly hurt, and with a huge sucking wound in his back he knew his time was limited. He managed a few words with Sergeant David Christie who had been instrumental in recovering him, under fire, on a stretcher:

'*Jock, I'm dying. Tell my wife I love her and go and see her for me.*[4]'

The field grave of Trooper Edmond, Recce Squadron, who was killed in the German ambush. Taylor Library

He was buried the next day. The following day Trooper Minns was recovered from a ditch still alive and was taken prisoner. He survived the war.

If you want to obtain an enemy view of the action go up onto the mound to the left of the track and look back on the ambush site. It is still possible to find old German trenches there.

The ambush that took place by the railway was to have far-reaching consequences. At its height, Freddie Gough had been called to see Urquhart. The reason, unknown to Gough, was to discuss his missing vehicles, which, of course, were not missing. However, he was pulled away at a vital time for the squadron. Having recovered, as best they could it's casualties, the Squadron then withdrew and abandoned its attempt to reach the Bridge. Sepp Krafft, with just a platoon north of the railway, had prevented a key part of the British divisional plan from being carried out.

There were a number of other things that happened in this general area. Stand on the track, with the tunnel immediately on your right and facing the motorway bridge. This track featured in many plans, not

A Willys Jeep in the tunnel ('10 Para Culvert') under the railway, driven by the author, supervised by Robert N Sigmond.

only those of the Reconnaissance Squadron. It was also the approach march of 7 KOSB, for once they had seen 4th Parachute Brigade safely down on South Ginkel Heath they were to secure the LZ for the Polish equipment gliders for day three; and LZ 'L' is just over one kilometre ahead of where you are standing, and slightly left of the track.

Four kilometres from where you are standing, and again just left of the track, is a 4th Brigade objective en route to its final planned position in Arnhem. The track, therefore, was also the approach march on 18 September, the second day, for 156 Parachute Battalion, the leading 4th Brigade battalion, and for 10th Parachute Battalion which very soon shifted some way over to the left moving through the woods to the north, following Amsterdamseweg as planned.

The battle in which 4th Parachute Brigade was involved on day three took place about three kilometres ahead and is described in Chapter 3. However, by mid-afternoon on 19 September 1944 the Brigade, by then comprising 156 and 10th Parachute Battalions and 7 KOSB, was withdrawing back through this area towards the Wolfheze level crossing with a view to moving south of the railway embankment and taking up a position in the defensive perimeter by then forming around Oosterbeek. The level crossing itself was being mortared, so many of the men sought to cross the embankment by climbing it, and a number went through the tunnel just by where you are standing. Nick-named by some the '10 Para Culvert', its use was by no means limited to men of that battalion. Its particular value was for the passage of vehicles: it is perfectly possible to drive a Willys Jeep through the tunnel towing a trailer or a 6-pounder anti-tank gun. One simply needs to drop the windscreen.

**The King's Own
Scottish Borders.**

The scene on that afternoon was one approaching chaos. The Brigade was conducting that most difficult of military operations: a withdrawal in contact with the enemy. As it did so the gliders carrying the Polish equipment were landing on LZ 'L' mixing in amongst British soldiers rushing, many of them in small groups, to get to the south side of the railway. The Germans were hotly pursuing them, and in the confusion there were a number of casualties, some, reportedly, as a result of 'friendly' fire between the British and their Polish allies. The embankment was presenting a difficult barrier. It is very steep, and to tired, overloaded men it was, in many cases, too much. For those who

Private Robin Holburn KOSB.
Courtesy R N Sigmond.

did get to the top and sought to cross there was the gauntlet of enemy machine-gun fire to be run as the Germans sprayed the railway line constantly along the line of the embankment. Many died and many were taken prisoner.

Private Robin Holburn of the Mortar Group, Support Company 7 KOSB was caught up in the melee:

'The troops coming from the Landing Zone were a mix of units including, I seem to recall, 10th Parachute Battalion. Whilst moving along the track I passed two anti-tank guns lying on their sides and recall thinking that we could not afford to 'lose' these. At a point about half way between Johannahoeve Farm the confusion became pronounced with the general movement of soldiers climbing the railway embankment. There were instances of jeeps trying to get up the embankment which now appeared to be the general line of withdrawal. No one was moving towards Wolfheze. Everyone was climbing the embankment and crossing the railway. Our mortar team, using toggle ropes, endeavoured to manhandle the handcart up the embankment but were unable to do so. We rested for a moment before trying again. At this point I was called over to assist a Jeep which had been trying to climb the embankment, this was not possible. We managed to get the Jeep back on the track where it moved towards Wolfheze. I returned to the mortars, but no one was there. It suddenly became quiet. A few soldiers were climbing still over the embankment, but were well scattered, no other movement was apparent along the track. I followed over the railway embankment and found myself alone on the south side in a heavily wooded area.[5]'

Leave this scene that once witnessed so much confusion and return in your car back along the track to the Wolfheze level crossing. **Turn right,** heading north along Wolfhezerweg. In a short distance you break clear of trees and there is a large open area to your left and right, with the majority to your left. This is LZ 'S'. **Stop as soon as you can** on the right of the road and remain in your car from where this part of the area is safest viewed.

This is the route taken initially by Lieutenant Colonel Dobie and the 1st Parachute Battalion. The Ede-Amsterdam road is about two kilometres ahead of you, running across your front at ninety degrees and he was to march to the junction and turn right towards Arnhem.

However, we are here to consider the scene on LZ 'S' which was a mirror of LZ 'Z', but remember that those descending onto LZ 'S' had been the first to land. Coming in from your right and flying overhead where you are parked, by now down to about 200 feet, the first gliders would land at the far end of the LZ. Looking into the distance it should be possible to see a grey-roofed building. This is Reijerskamp Farm, a main focus on the DZ as well as being the HQ of the 21st Independent Parachute Company. Some of the problems encountered, however, were the same, as witness the experiences of Lance Corporal George Hynd of the 7 KOSB Pioneer Platoon:

> 'The platoon I was in went over in different gliders. In my glider were also one Jeep and two trailers loaded with explosives and pioneer equipment... After landing the fun started right away! We just couldn't get the Jeep or trailers out. Both glider pilots, Fawler and Mitchell, did assist us. However, out of the woods came civilians who were keen to help us and with their combined effort we got the glider unloaded.[6']

One key difference was that the arrival of a Scottish battalion heralded the presence of the pipes. As the soldiers set about sorting out the LZ and moving of to their task of defending DZ 'Y' for the next day they were encouraged in their

Piper Willie Ford, who would have been dressed as an Airborne soldier and not in his ceremonial accoutrements as shown here.
Courtesy R N Sigmond.

work by Piper Willie Ford from Selkirk, playing the Battalion march – *Blue Bonnets O'er The Border* – at the top end of the LZ.

Dobie's men of 1st Parachute Battalion marched past here towards the road junction ahead, marked today by traffic lights, with a view to turning right and heading towards Arnhem. However, the Germans were too fast and they already had men of the 9th SS with light armoured vehicles in position. They were there to seek out the paratroopers, and had no idea that a complete British battalion was approaching them.

Drive on towards the junction, and just before the start of a wood on your right and about 200 metres short of the junction is a track leading off to the right, and it is easy to park across the entrance. In trying to picture the scene in 1944, the only real change has been the Ede-Arnhem road. It is now a wide dual carriageway, but in 1944 it was a normal two-way road taking the space currently occupied by the northern carriageway, furthest from you. The nearest, southern, carriageway, signed Arnhem, is a post-war construction. This means that the woods, whilst being of similar density, are not so extensive as they were.

The junction of Wolfhezerweg with the Amsterdam-Ede road. Park by the track junction on the right. Courtesy Drs Robert P G A Voskuil

It was in these woods that the Battalion fought its first battle. The leading company was soon embroiled with the enemy and fighting continued for several hours, until it became dark which made the engaging of targets virtually impossible. German armoured vehicles fired their machine-guns into the advancing soldiers. The British quickly began to take cover, and to dig themselves small scrapes in the earth, using their entrenching tools whilst lying down in order to obtain as much protection as they could whilst at the same time having a good position from which to return fire. Andrew Milbourne was the leader, known as the 'No 1', on a Vickers machine-gun team.

'Shells began to burst amongst us. Yells and whistles filled the air and machine-guns opened fire. I noticed before I hugged the ground that one of the enemy guns was about 200 yards in front and to our left flank. My officer asked if I had seen anything and when I pointed the gun out to him ordered my gun section into action. Grasping the tripod I ran across the road, diving headlong into a very convenient ditch. Cautiously I raised my head looking for a position for my gun. Before having completed my look round No 2 landed on top of me. "You bloody awkward elephant", I began to curse, then stopped. A burst of fire was spraying the ditch... Finally I reached my position and slowly spread-eagled the tripod legs. Then, raising it slightly to the required height for a low mounting, I clamped the legs tight. Shuffling round I yelled for No 2. Slowly he approached and as he did so I ordered No 3 to get near enough to supply us with ammunition. At last, after what seemed an age, No 2 reached my side and mounted the gun.[7]

Eventually, in the dark, the situation became chaotic with Germans now all around and the airborne suffering constant bombardment from mortars, tank guns and machine-guns. Andrew Milbourne again:

'We were swept by withering fire. Dead lay all around, wounded were crying for water. Groans and shrieks of pain filled the air. Time and again they overran our positions and had to be driven out with the bayonet. My gun was never out of action.[8]

Eventually, Dobie decided that he had to get away, and instead of taking the Ede-Arnhem road, now denied to him, he began to move away through the woods to the right of where you are now parked, still intending to head for his objective. It was only later that evening, at about 8.00 pm, that he picked up a garbled radio message from the Bridge, realised that Frost was in trouble and decided to head south-east into Oosterbeek and then on to Arnhem to help out at the Bridge. By dawn the next morning he would be well into Oosterbeek, but with severely reduced numbers. Two companies had sustained around thirty casualties each, and another was down to half strength. A number of men had simply become lost in the confusion. Some would be taken prisoner and others would turn up, many hours later, in Oosterbeek.

Drive on to the junction and turn left, signed **Ede**. You are now heading in the direction of the 4th Parachute Brigade DZ. As a reminder, keep thinking about distances as you cross the motorway bridge and head towards the woods on the other side towards South Ginkel Heath; DZ 'Y'. It was the task of 7 KOSB to guard the heath, but their orders, worked out from a map and photographs in England, were that they should ambush the road to the DZ to prevent interference by the enemy. Consequently, 'A' Company 7 KOSB, twenty-five percent of the Battalion's rifle strength, was instructed to set up an ambush by a restaurant called 'Planken Wambuis', which means, literally 'Wooden Skirt, or 'Coffin'. It is on the left shortly after you enter the woods, and you can stop in the car park; and your trip meter should read **10.8 miles/17.3 km**.

Private Bill Anderson of 1 Platoon, A Company describes what happened:

'We proceeded to a slight bend in the road and we were told by our officer, Lieutenant Kane, a Canadian, to stop everything on this

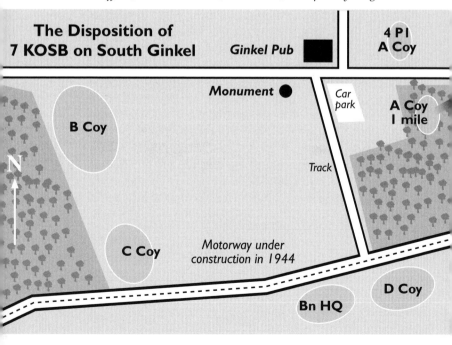

The Disposition of
7 KOSB on South Ginkel

Ginkel Pub

4 Pl
A Coy

Monument ●

Car park

A Coy
I mile

B Coy

N

Track

C Coy

Motorway under
construction in 1944

D Coy

Bn HQ

road. Some time later we heard engines and from Ede way an ambulance and a truck went by, but no one fired a shot! Lieutenant Kane shouted: 'why did no one fire?' I don't know, but someone said one was an ambulance. So Kane repeated the order to stop everything. Once again more traffic drove up. Another ambulance and a small pick-up truck which we fired at and stopped both. The truck had two occupants who were bleeding terribly and the ambulance when the door opened was full of armed Germans with rifles. The German occupants were taken prisoner. During the night heavy fighting was taking place nearer to Arnhem and the noise was terrible.'

Move on to South Ginkel Heath, which is about a mile further on. As you do so, bear in mind 4 Platoon of A Company that was sent along the road down which you are now driving to establish itself between the battalion and A Company to form some kind of link. The logic and the reasons are unclear, but presumably it may have had something to do with the range of radios. However, the move also deprived A Company of 25% of its firepower. Carrying on along the road and shortly after clearing the woods there is a pub on the right called the Ginkel. **Opposite** there is an entrance to a car park into which you should turn, trip meter reading **11.8 miles/18.9 km**. Leave the car and proceed on foot to the mound under the tree on the corner of the heath. Here you will find a memorial to the men who landed here and to those who defended the LZ.

As you cleared the woods you passed the place, somewhere on the right of the road, where 4 Platoon, A Company, took up its position. The area can be clearly seen from where you are standing, and is marked

The memorial to 4 Brigade, 7 KOSB and the Dutch Resistance. It is located at the 10th Parachute Battalion RV. The Ginkel Pub is in the background.

on the sketch map on Page 60.

Stand with your back to the monument and look out across the heath. In the far distance there is a tree line where runs a modern motorway, impossible to see from here. Under construction during the battle, it marks the southern edge of the DZ. The Ede-Arnhem road behind you is the northern edge, whilst the track running away south from the car park on your left is the eastern edge. Look to your right and away in the distance can be seen the line of a large wood, marking the western edge.

Positioned to defend the western edge and to be in a position to bring fire to bear on enemy approaching along the road from Ede was B Company of 7 KOSB. Further south where the motorway enters the tree line was C Company. Battalion HQ and D Company were at the bottom, south-eastern corner. D Company was the Battalion's reserve, and was missing a platoon whose glider had not made it to the LZ. It would eventually arrive with the second lift. However, at this critical time D Company was without 25% of its firepower. A Company's position you have already passed at the Planken Wambuis. This was a vast area of responsibility for a single battalion, and especially one with no inherent mobility. Furthermore, look at the distance of the A Company 'link', namely 4 Platoon, from where Battalion HQ was positioned, and perhaps wonder briefly how the link was to be established given the distances you have travelled and seen.

The main events here took place on the second day. However, the KOSB actually arrived on the evening of the first day and consequently had to endure a night's attention from Germans who were keen that the British should not prevail. The outcome was that they lost a number of men. Perhaps not surprisingly, the detached 4 Platoon was eliminated with only a few of its members making their way back to their company the next morning. There was also some activity by the track that marks the eastern edge of the DZ where, about half way along, there were some workers huts in 1944. It was in this area that 16 Platoon of D Company had been positioned on the evening of 17 September. However, during the night and early morning German activity saw those of the platoon who were not killed taken prisoner. D Company was down to just two platoons as the Battalion prepared for the main event of the second day: the arrival of 4th Parachute Brigade on South Ginkel Heath.

However, the Germans had been given time to prepare, surprise had gone, the paratroopers were expected. What had given it away, at least in part, was the presence of a defensive force protecting this area.

Clearly there for a reason and the reason could only be, so ran the German logic, further airborne landings. From the west General von Tettau's hastily formed battlegroups were advancing, and from the north a Dutch SS battalion with its HQ in the Ginkel pub was causing trouble for the defenders. At the same time, the Germans were throwing up defences between the landing zones and Arnhem itself. By 3.00 pm on 18 September the odds were approximately fourteen German to six British battalions, not including tanks, artillery and heavy infantry weapons which the Germans had in preponderance. This considerable weight of military capability had formed a box into which 4th Parachute Brigade was about to drop.

The KOSB were under attack when they saw in the distance the small dots, growing ever larger, which heralded the arrival of the force they had been expecting for some time. Delayed in take off due to mist in England, the Brigade was on its way in. The KOSB, having fought off German probes all night, now swept across the area in a final counter attack that would clear, as far as possible, the DZ. Lance Corporal Tom Smith, an anti-tank gunner with the KOSB, recalls what happened:

'At 3.00 pm we heard a mighty roar and all hell broke loose. We were ordered to fix bayonets and chase the Germans from the zone so, when the piper began to drone, we did that and they ran like hell.'

Counter-attacked from the ground, and assaulted from the air, the Dutch SS battalion broke and ran. However, there were enough German soldiers in the vicinity to pour a considerable weight of fire into the paratroopers as they landed and whilst still in the air. Many were wounded or killed before landing. Tracer and mortar bombs also set the heather alight and fires were raging all over the DZ, smoke adding to the confusion. At least one wounded soldier was heard

Dutch volunteers serving in the SS fought with varying degrees of effectiveness.

An example of a 20mm Flak gun mounted on half track. Alerted to the second drop the Germans were able to put up a withering fire on the transports and falling pararoopers of 4 Parachute Brigade.

screaming as the flames reached him, and then his ammunition exploded.

The Brigade Commander, Brigadier Shan Hackett, was one of the first to land, and in doing so lost his walking stick. He found it eventually, having also found ten Germans who wished to surrender. Brandishing the stick, he marched them off to his headquarters. As he moved to his RV so did the units, 10th Battalion's being near the memorial where you are standing. Landing for at least one person, however, was unexpected. Tom Smith again:

'A para landed smack on our position. We helped him to his feet; he looked very young and sort of dazed, as if he was wondering what the hell he was doing here. We noted that he wasn't armed or equipped. My officer asked him "why". This is what he said: "I shouldn't be here. I am on a forty-eight hour pass, I volunteered to push the supplies from the Dakotas because I had never flown before." He was in the RASC. The Dakota was shot down. We equipped him from a dead man. The officer said: "your leave has been cancelled, and you are now in the KOSB. Your NCO is Corporal McKay". I never saw him again, or knew his name or if he survived the battle. We pissed ourselves at the expression on his face.'

The previous day, shortly after landing, General Urquhart had gone forward with 1st Parachute Brigade to assess the situation. He had been cut off and had been out of touch since then. Brigadier Philip Hicks of the Airlanding Brigade, standing in as Divisional Commander, had decided that the assault on the Bridge in Arnhem needed additional resources. He had therefore decided to detach Hackett's 11th Parachute Battalion for this task, and to do so as soon as it arrived on the DZ. The first Hackett learned of this was on landing. He was not best pleased, and so having consolidated his brigade, it was with only two of his three battalions that he moved eastwards in the direction of his objectives north of Arnhem. He had arranged to have 7 KOSB in his brigade to make up for the loss, but their task was to protect the Polish LZ 'L' for the landing the next day, and that was to be their primary task for the time being.

So, with the blocking lines moving into place, the formation of more and more German battlegroups, difficulties in Arnhem as the bulk of 1st Parachute Brigade, the divisional commander missing, was being prevented from reaching the Bridge and command and control muddles between the brigadiers, it was not looking good for the airborne soldiers. However, that would be to underplay the effect of the 4th Brigade landing on the Germans. The battalion ratio had now adjusted to fourteen German to nine British, and this further manifestation of Allied power had caused many to wonder if the assault was not unstoppable. SS-*Hauptsturmführer* Wilfried Schwartz summed up the view held by many in 9th SS *Hohenstaufen* Division:

'In Normandy...we were too late. In Arnhem we were too few! How were we to stop this elite airborne division?[10]'

Returning to your car **drive back the way you came**. As you leave, bear in mind that 4th Brigade's heavy equipment had landed on LZ 'X', which is some five miles or 8 kilometres away by road, although closer using a direct, cross-country, route. All this would need to marry up before the Brigade was properly resourced.

Turn right at the junction leading back down to the Wolfheze level crossing. Drive past the Johannahoeveweg junction, over the crossing and **carry straight on**. As you do, glance to the right and view the Wolfheze psychiatric hospital. It was rebuilt after the war having been bombed prior to the battle by the Americans on the instructions of the British. It was believed, quite erroneously, that it was a base for German soldiers and hence a threat to the landings.

As you **drive on down** Wolfhezerweg you have Sepp Krafft's blocking position with his two forward companies in the woods to your left. It was from here that he sent out his initial spoiling patrols, and it was a line he held until about 9.00 pm on the first evening. When you reach the junction with Utrechtseweg **turn left** and after a few metres **turn left** again onto a track called Bredelaan at which is also the entrance to the Hotel Bilderberg and by now the trip meter should read **19.1 miles/30.6 km**. Find a safe place to stop and leave your car. **Return to Utrechtseweg** and find a place where you can safely look left and right. To your right is the Wolfhezerweg junction, and to your left one kilometre away is the Koude (Oude) Herberg crossroads, the crossroads/roundabout you crossed at the start of this tour, and beyond that the Hartenstein. Remember, on South Ginkel Heath at the 4th Brigade landings we were discussing events on Day 2. Now we are back on Day one.

Utrechtseweg was the central route for the 1st Parachute Brigade advance on the first day, the one taken by 3rd Parachute Battalion. Having left the DZ at 3.00 pm the lead elements had arrived at the point where you are standing at around 5.00 pm. Bear in mind that a battalion strung out on a tactical march filled about a mile of road. The Arnhem town commandant, Major General Kussin, had been visiting Krafft's battalion HQ at the Wolfheze Hotel, near the level crossing, trying to find out what was going on, and to give orders to Krafft. In planning his route back to Arnhem, he declined Krafft's advice to take the Bilderberglaan.

'I have no time to spare,[11]' said the general driving down Wolfhezerweg, making for the faster route into town. He reached the junction at the same time as the lead platoon of 3rd Parachute Battalion.

Lieutenant James Cleminson was the platoon commander:

'...owing to the high garden fences all that we could do was to string out on either side of the road and keep moving as fast as possible. There was no real opposition, but as we approached the crossroads a German staff car swept down the road from Wolfheze into the middle of my front section. We were all keyed up, so everyone let fly at it, stopping it dead and killing all the occupants. We pushed on leaving Company HQ to clear it up.[12]'

In the woods behind the Bilderberg Hotel was Sepp Krafft's left-forward company. Shortly after the Kussin incident they brought mortar and machine-gun fire down onto the advancing paratroopers in the area where you are now standing. It was about now that General Urquhart appeared. Seeking to encourage a swift advance, and being out of touch with events because of failures in the radio communications he had gone along the southern route to push the

General Kussin, the Arnhem town commandant, was killed in an encounter with 3rd Parachute Battalion. TAYLOR LIBRARY

Brigade Commander to redouble his efforts. However, Lathbury had been no longer on the southern route. As anxious as his Divisional Commander for the impetus to be kept going he was on the central route encouraging 3rd Battalion, so when Urquhart arrived on the scene as well, Lieutenant Colonel J A C Fitch, the Commanding Officer, was faced with both his Brigade and Divisional Commanders peering over his shoulder every time he made a decision. Not a happy state of affairs, especially since both commanders were now out of touch with

The scene of General Kussin's death, looking at the junction from the opposite side of Utrechtseweg.

The spot where Kussin met his death.

their respective HQs. The Division and its lead Brigade were now leaderless.

Lieutenant Colonel Fitch's response to Krafft's attack was swift and positive. He ordered Major Mervyn Dennison's A Company to clear the opposition so as to allow the battalion to get on. Major Dennison describes what happened in a battle that took place in the grounds of the Bilderberg hotel:

> 'I sent Lieutenant Ashe's platoon to the north to locate the mortars which were still bringing fire down on us. I then moved off with Lieutenant Baxter's platoon to give support on the left. A German OP on a water tower which was obviously directing the fire was attacked and destroyed. The platoons swept on through the mortar position and destroyed it and some heavy machine guns. About twenty Germans were killed or wounded and another eighteen taken prisoner. We lost some twenty casualties, mostly wounded. It was just after dark before my company joined the rest of the battalion.'[13]

To allow you to orientate your position, Bredelaan in which you are standing, faces northwards.

Once Krafft's forward company had been cleared and had moved away, the Battalion attempted to continue down Utrechtseweg. They had not gone far when a self-propelled gun met them. Whilst working out how best to cope with this new problem, Peter Waddy, B Company commander, and Lieutenant Cleminson saw a 6-pounder anti-tank gun detachment draw up. Being towed by a jeep, the gun was facing the wrong way to deal with an armoured vehicle to its front. Both officers were alarmed at the 'casual' manner in which the gun crew began to deploy their gun to deal with the threat. They were not fast enough: the Germans put a high explosive round down into the road just in front of the 6-pounder where it exploded killing or wounding the crew, although the gun was later recovered by another jeep. Equally surprising was the subsequent action of the German mobile gun. It drove down to the wreckage, a crew member alighted, picked up a wounded anti-tank gunner and draped him over the front glacis plate of the vehicle as protection from British fire. He then climbed back into his vehicle and withdrew, with the British not being prepared to fire on him for fear of hitting one of their own soldiers.

The advance resumed, and the leading elements were by now near the Koude (Oude) Herberg crossroads. But soon more armoured

SS soldiers riding on a Hummel self-propelled gun. This serves as an example of the sort of opposition the lightly armed airborne troops were facing (though not taken at Arnhem). TAYLOR LIBRARY

vehicles appeared, and Lieutenant Colonel Fitch decided to send C Company up Bredelaan, where your car is parked, in an attempt to 'find an open route to the Bridge'. Len Wright was to take the lead with his 9 Platoon, and was giving orders to the key NCOs in his platoon when Brigadier Lathbury appeared on the scene, seeking out the leading platoon commander. In a scene typical of the sort of thing that happens when senior officers get involved where they ought not to be, Lathbury brusquely curtailed the giving of orders and told Len in no uncertain terms to get going. Remembering to salute, Len said:

'Sergeant Mason, get them going. I'll brief you on the move.' With that they dashed into Bredelaan and led the company away. That was the last they were to see of the Battalion, or the Battalion of them.

C Company, after some adventures, was eventually to make it to the Arnhem Bridge. Moving up Bredelaan it turned right along the railway, and eventually emerged in the town at the main railway station before making its way down to Frost's position where it arrived, somewhat the worse for wear and at less than half strength, in the early hours of Monday morning.

The presence of more armour to his front caused Lieutenant Colonel Fitch to consider his position and, in company with the two senior officers, he chose to stay where he was until first light the next morning. It was a decision often since criticised, for the Battalion was relatively fresh and very many who were there, of all ranks, felt, and still feel, they should have moved on. The next morning instead of continuing down Utrechtseweg they moved just past the Hartenstein in order to avoid German opposition and then down to the bottom road in an attempt to get to the Bridge. They were never to make it, but that is another part of the story for another time.

Return to your car and proceed back towards the Hartenstein from where you can either continue with the next tour or perhaps pause for refreshment. Before you do, however, you might like to walk a little way towards the Wolfhezerweg junction and spare a look to the right at the house at **No 269** Utrechtseweg. This is where Urquhart and Lathbury spent the night of 17 September 1944.

[1] From *'When Dragons Flew – An Illustrated History of the 1st Battalion The Border Regiment 1939-45'* by Stuart Eastwood, Charles Gray and Alan Green, The Regimental Museum The Border Regiment in association with Silver Link Publishing Ltd, Peterborough 1994.

[2] From *'First In! Parachute Pathfinder Company'* by Ron Kent, B Batsford Ltd, London, and Hippocrene Books, New York, 1979.

[3] From *'Remember Arnhem'* by John Fairley, Peaton Press, Glasgow 1978.

[4] *ibid*

[5] From *'Off At Last – An Illustrated History of the 7th (Galloway) Battalion The King's Own Scottish Borderers 1939 – 1945'* by Robert Sigmond, 1997.

[6] *ibid*

[7] From *'Arnhem'* by Christopher Hibbert, B T Batsford Ltd, London, 1962.

[8] *ibid*

[9] From *'Off At Last'* by Robert Sigmond, 1997.

[10] From *'It Never Snows in September'* by Robert J Kershaw, The Crowood Press, 1990

[11] From *'Airborne Carpet: Operation Market Garden'* by Anthony Farrar-Hockley, MacDonald and Co, 1970.

[12] From *'A Tour Of The Arnhem Battlefields'* by John Waddy, Pen and Sword Books Limited, 1999.

[13] *ibid*

CHAPTER THREE

4TH BRIGADE'S FIRST BATTLE
AND THE NORTHERN PERIMETER

Duration – Two hours by car
Distance – 7.4 miles or 11.9 Kilometres

Set the trip meter once more to zero and from the car park behind the Kleyn Hartensteyn move to Utrechtseweg, **turning right** this time to the crossroads 100 metres away and **then left**, following the signs to the Commonwealth War Graves Commission cemetery. This is Stationsweg. As you drive along the British 'front line' was, largely, in the houses on your left, and the Germans' on the right. Distance is again a feature of our tour, for the ranges and fields of fire along here, as in so many other places, were incredibly short.

Note again the fences and hedges, seriously limiting movement for both sides. Street fighting is always an intense, difficult and dangerous undertaking; and here it was made all the more so by the inability tactically to deploy easily outside the houses. Think also of the men defending the buildings to your left. As you pass Paul Krugerstraat on your left the next few buildings were held from Wednesday afternoon by 156 Parachute Battalion, by then down to less than fifty men and commanded by Major Geoffrey Powell. On beyond that, around Cronjéweg, the Reconnaissance Squadron was defending the perimeter.

From this point on the edge of the perimeter begins to move away from Stationsweg to the left forming the curve around the northern edge of what was called by some the 'Oosterbeek Thumb', with its base on the north bank of the Rhine. Very shortly you will cross the Oosterbeek railway bridge, known in 1944 as Oosterbeek Hoog. Ignore, for the time being, the right turn to the Cemetery, for we shall return here later. Opposite that road, on your left, is a minor road, almost a track, leading away to the west. That is Johannahoeveweg, and you will remember entering at the other end when visiting the Reconnaissance Squadron ambush and the '10 Para Culvert'. Had the Reconnaissance Squadron been able to proceed unhindered they would have emerged along that track. It is here also that C Company of 3rd Parachute Battalion emerged on the first night, following the line of the railway on their way into Arnhem. Today it is no longer possible to cover the whole of the route as it is blocked in the middle.

Drive straight on up the main road, now called Dreijenseweg. It is along here that SS-Sturmbannführer Spindler had begun to form one of his blocking positions as early as the evening of Sunday 17 September, holding the ground and the houses to the right of the road. Ahead you

71

can see the road flanked by woods, but before you enter the trees glance to your right and note that the ground slopes upwards. The hill about 500 metres to the right is the Lichtenbeek feature, and was 4th Parachute Brigade's initial objective. Once secured it would provide a base for its advance on Arnhem.

As you enter the darkness of the wood remember to abide by the local traffic advice and use dipped headlights, even on the brightest day. Imagine the situation on 19 September, when 4th Brigade bumped Spindler's blocking line in its attempt to reach the first objective. The Germans were dug in on the right, among the trees and uphill from the advancing paratroopers. The airborne, on the other hand, advancing from your left and from lower down the slope, were exposed to a well armed, well supplied, well supported enemy who had been granted the opportunity to entrench a strong position, with infantry supported by heavy machine guns, mortars and armoured vehicles.

Just over one kilometre from the railway bridge, with the trip meter reading **1.5 miles/2.4 kilometers**, you will see ahead of you the traffic lights on the junction with the main Ede-Arnhem road. About twenty metres before it there is on the left a minor road, Sportlaan, signed to St Jozefhuis Mill Hill. **Turn left** and find **a place to park** a couple of hundred metres down this road, allowing plenty of room for the odd passing car. In doing so you will have the woods on your right, with the Ede-Arnhem road beyond them; and you will be able to hear the traffic noise. On your left will be a large open expanse with a line of woods on the far side. Looking ahead you will be able to make out the end of this open area by the line of trees along a road that marks its western end. The scene of the Reconnaissance Squadron ambush is about two kilometres beyond that line of trees, almost exactly due west of where you are positioned. In this area we shall be examining the fate of three infantry battalions, beginning with 7 KOSB.

Drive along the road towards the western end of the open area. At the end is a crossroads faced by a high fence and a gate. **Park** safely wherever you can.

Facing the fence and the line of the track leading through it, LZ 'L' is just on the other side of the trees, slightly to your right. It is an area currently occupied by a sports complex and golf club.

Having completed its task of defending South Ginkel Heath for the 4 Brigade drop, 7 KOSB moved off in the evening of 18 September onto its next task: protection of LZ 'L' in anticipation of the landing of gliders with the Polish heavy equipment on 19 September. As they moved along Johannahoeveweg, B Company was in the lead. Look up to the left, as if you had turned left at the crossroads where you are standing, and you will see Johannahoeve Farm, now occupied by the Mill Hill Fathers. B Company came along the track leading in to the

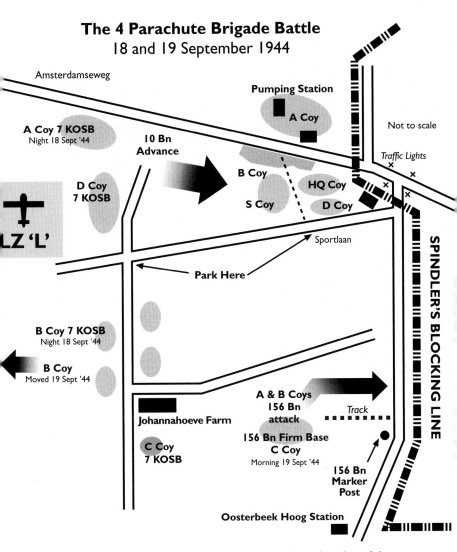

The 4 Parachute Brigade Battle
18 and 19 September 1944

Amsterdamseweg

Pumping Station

A Coy

Not to scale

A Coy 7 KOSB
Night 18 Sept '44

10 Bn
Advance

Traffic Lights

B Coy

D Coy
7 KOSB

HQ Coy

S Coy

D Coy

LZ 'L'

Sportlaan

Park Here

SPINDLER'S BLOCKING LINE

B Coy 7 KOSB
Night 18 Sept '44

B Coy
Moved 19 Sept '44

A & B Coys
156 Bn
attack

Track

Johannahoeve Farm

156 Bn Firm Base
C Coy
Morning 19 Sept '44

C Coy
7 KOSB

156 Bn
Marker
Post

Oosterbeek Hoog Station

farm area from your right and then made its way along the edge of the
wood leading away to your left towards Dreijenseweg about one
kilometre away. Looking along the line of the wood you will see some
white farm buildings about half way down.

B Company of 7 KOSB had orders to proceed to a point, 54.2, some
500 metres beyond the Dreijenseweg, which seems odd when the
battalion's role was protection of the LZ just near you. However, the
white farm buildings mark the rough area that was about as far as they
got in the dark of the Monday night. Major Michael Forman was the

Company Commander:

> '...we came under heavy and close range fire in complete darkness. The grounds on the left of the track and in front of us were open and we deployed to the right side of the track. Further Spandau and 20mm machine-gun fire came from the Dreijenseweg in front of us. We were pinned down in a fierce firefight which must have lasted three-quarters of an hour in a sea of brushwood from recently felled pine trees. We were then ordered...to withdraw to Johannahoeve Farm, which we did under uncomfortable fire as it was by then getting light. Regrettably, Donald Murray and some three or four others were killed in this encounter. Corporal McCleary stayed to the last to cover our withdrawal with a Bren gun and we ran back together encouraged by 20mm tracer bullets. We dug in at Johannahoeve Farm crossroads and along the track to the north and were duly mortared by the enemy but without casualties, as we had our breakfast.'[1]

That crossroads, more of a cross track, is up by the farm buildings which are south of where you are standing and Michael Forman's company was strung out, dug in, with all four platoons on either side of the narrow road leading away from you towards the farm. C Company was in the woods beyond the farm. If you look the other way, as if you had turned right at the crossroads, you will see a bend in the road about 500 metres away. It is here that D Company was dug in. Beyond D Company's position, roughly in line with where you are standing, A Company was in a position on the main Ede-Arnhem road, and you can hear the traffic from where you are. You will remember A Company was isolated at Planken Wambuis during the defence of DZ 'Y'; and here it was, isolated again.

To help with orientation, Sportlaan runs east-west and the road to the right at your present position leading to D Company's position faces northwards.

At 0740 on 19 September Brigadier Hackett informed the KOSB CO, Lieutenant Colonel Robert Payton-Reid, that his battalion was now under his command as part of 4 Brigade. His orders were that the Battalion had to hold a firm base on its present position and carry out its pre-arranged task of protecting LZ 'L'. He was also informed that 156 Parachute Battalion would advance through his left southern flank, and 10th Parachute Battalion along the right northern flank. To secure the position Payton-Reid moved B Company from the area in which you are standing and sited them about 700 metres due west in order to protect the south and west sides of the LZ.

As you imagine them around you, sorting equipment, checking guns and preparing for their move on foot, **return to your car and drive back** towards the Dreijenseweg. Shortly before you reach the end of the woods, a couple of hundred metres, you will see a track leading into the woods to your left, with an electricity transformer about 50 metres into the trees. **Park here**, and position yourself by the fence on the right where you can obtain a good all-round view.

Hackett's plan for 4 Brigade was to advance on the morning of Tuesday 19 September, with 156 Battalion on the right assaulting the enemy. The Battalion had tried to get through the night before, as had 7 KOSB, but had also been pushed back by German resistance in roughly the same area. Moving forward again, its objective was to take a piece of high ground near the corner of the woods just as you entered them in your car driving up from Oosterbeek. From where you are this is on the other side of the woods immediately to your front on the other side of the field, and we shall take a closer look later on. By the time it made its second attempt at 0700 on the Tuesday, the Germans had withdrawn and the objective was clear. Geoffrey Powell's C Company occupied it without resistance. The plan then was that the other two companies would move to the left, through the woods whose edge you see from where you are standing, across the Dreijenseweg to your left and on to the high ground some 500 metres on the other side.

The 10th Parachute Battalion was to hold a firm position on the

Brigadier Shan Hackett.

The German Spandau or MG 34 machine-gun. It was one of the most rapid firing and reliable guns of its time. It featured an air cooled barrel and was belt fed with up to 250 rounds of 7.92 mm bullets in a belt.

main Ede-Arnhem road. If you turn round and face the road, beyond the woods slightly to your right are the traffic lights near where you turned into this minor road. Sweeping round to the left imagine about three-quarters of a mile from there along the road and that is where they were supposed to be. However, Lieutenant Colonel Smyth, having reached that point by about 10.00 am, began to move towards Arnhem through the woods immediately in front of you and approaching from the left of where you are standing. When picturing the area in 1944 remember that the Ede-Arnhem road, called Amsterdamseweg, was then only as wide as a single carriageway on the modern road, and that it was the part nearest to you that was built up after the war. The woods in front of you were, therefore, a little more extensive in those days.

D Company, commanded by Captain Mike Horsfall, was in the lead. It was in the woods just to the right of where you are standing that they hit Spindler's line, and in particular an array of machine-guns and armoured vehicles clustered in the area of De Leeren Doedel, the restaurant by the petrol station at the traffic light. His immediate reaction, and in accordance with the standard procedure, was to return enemy fire as hard as he could, whilst seeking to outflank the opposition from within his company's resources. He sent a platoon across Amsterdamseweg, but the platoon commander could not cope with the opposition. Lieutenant Colonel Smyth in battalion HQ soon realised what was happening and sought permission from Hackett to try outflanking with a larger force. For some reason he was limited by Hackett's headquarters to using no more than a company. With two rifle companies now closed up on each other and, under fire in the

Captain L. E. Queripel

woods right in front of you, he chose Captain Lionel Queripel's A Company at the rear and furthest from the enemy. Queripel was to base himself around the pumping station north of the main road and from there to turn what Smyth hoped was the German right flank and open the way for his battalion to move on towards Arnhem. However, Spindler's blocking line extended further north than had been thought and once again the Battalion's advance was repulsed.

During this action Lionel Queripel displayed the courage that would eventually lead to him becoming one of the five Arnhem VCs, and one of the decoration's four posthumous recipients. He demonstrated tremendous leadership, crossing and re-crossing the main road, once carrying a wounded sergeant, and always in the forefront of everything. The firepower being used against the lightly armed paratroopers was horrendous. In particular, the *Spandau* machine-gun, also called the MG34, was used to great effect. Long, grazing bursts were constantly fired mostly between knee and hip height, thereby keeping heads, and just about everything else, well down; and the Germans appeared to have a limitless supply of ammunition. The paratroopers, on the other hand, only had what they could carry.

As you can see from where you stand, the battalion was hemmed in to a narrow strip of woodland. To move out across either Amsterdamseweg or the road on which you are standing, was to attract a storm of fire that made any such moves dangerous in the extreme. Then, at 2.00 pm, and not having had any success in outflanking the Germans and wondering what his next move might be, the CO was ordered by Brigade HQ to withdraw back towards the Wolfheze level crossing. The reason was that a German force, Division von Tettau, was pushing hard from the west and there was a risk that the level crossing at Wolfheze would be taken. The railway embankment was, as you saw at the site of the Recce Squadron ambush, a real barrier, especially to vehicles, and with the Germans in possession of the only crossing point Hackett's brigade would be cut off. Since progress forward appeared unachievable he felt his only recourse was to withdraw south of the railway line.

So it was, unplanned and in great haste, that the 10th Battalion began that most difficult of military operations: a withdrawal in contact with the enemy. Most thinking people were aware of the difficulties this would cause, and the adjutant, when the orders were received, shouted to the CO:

'We can't withdraw from here – the Jerries are all around us.'
His CO's response was brisk and to the point:
'We've got our orders – let's get going.'

The route they were to take led across the fields from all around where you are standing, in the direction of Johannahoeve Farm and to its west, across the area of LZ 'L'. Imagine them running out from the woods and trying to make their way in small, uncoordinated groups across the open fields. For the German gunners, well dug in and with plentiful supplies of ammunition, it was a field day. Before long the open space in front of you and away beyond the crossroads where you last parked your car, was littered with dead and wounded paratroopers; and with the weight of fire many of those wounded and seeking still to get away were wounded two or three times, and sometimes even more. It was carnage, and it was during this withdrawal that Lionel Queripel won his VC, sacrificing his life that others might escape.

And just as they were in the middle of all this the Polish equipment gliders landed on LZ 'L', just beyond the crossroads where you were parked a few moments ago. Yet further chaos, as non-English speaking men in grey hats appeared amongst a Scottish Regiment defending their LZ and across which a parachute battalion, based, historically at least, on a Royal Sussex battalion was attempting to withdraw; and all of them being attacked by Germans. The gliders carried the Polish heavy equipment, such as their anti-tank guns. It was all supposed to marry up with the Polish parachute brigade due to land that day on the southern end of the Bridge in Arnhem. The brigade was delayed by bad weather that would keep it in England for another two days, so they were separated from their equipment. It didn't matter; most of it was destroyed in the chaos of the landing.

The other two battalions also withdrew, and in the process A Company of 7 KOSB was surrounded and made prisoner, less one platoon which managed to dodge away through the woods, but which fell into enemy hands the following morning.

We can now move to see the other 'half' of 4 Brigade's battle, to where 156 Parachute Battalion was engaged in the woods on the other side of the open space. **Go back** onto Dreijenseweg and **turn right back towards Oosterbeek**. Proceed to the edge of the woods and as you are about to exit into the open you will see a marker post on the right, a memorial to the events that happened here. Your trip meter should read some **3.5 miles/5.6 kilometers**. Pull over and **stop beside the marker**, there should be ample room to park.

Trying to describe the battle that took place here is beset with all the problems of describing any other action in battle. The historian is reliant upon the impressions of those present and they vary with perception and the passage of time. There are several accounts of what happened here, and they actually accord quite well as to the sequence of events and the outcome. However, precisely where it all happened is less clear and distances may be adrift by some tens of metres, extending to a hundred or so metres. This account is based for position around the only good map available, provided by Harry Bankhead of 156 Parachute Battalion as part of his book, to which a number of references are made in this guide. In seeking to describe events as many accounts of the action as possible have been incorporated.

Stand on the corner of the wood beside the road at a point where a track emerges onto the road from the west alongside the edge of the wood. Looking down Dreijenseweg towards the railway station there is a field in front of you to the right of the road. Look now to the right along the track as it follows the line of the wood to where it bends left after about 100 metres. From a point about half way round the bend in the track imagine a right turn, straight into the woods. Penetrating about 300 metres there is a knoll with another marker on it; and **you can walk to it** if you feel you have time. Allow a comfortable **twenty minutes**.

This was the 156 Parachute Battalion firm base occupied by C Company early on the morning of Tuesday 19 September 1944, and it was taken with barely a shot fired. Those Germans in the woods the night before, a sort of piquet line, had played their part by halting the advancing British in the dark of the previous night and had withdrawn behind the line of the Dreijenseweg to await their next attempt. With Geoffrey Powell's C Company secure Lieutenant Colonel Richard des Voeux pushed A Company around to its left to begin the assault on the high ground 500 metres beyond Dreijenseweg that was the Battalion's objective.

Walking carefully **back up Dreijenseweg** in the direction of the 10th Battalion battle you will come to **a track on your lef**t, after about 200 metres. Move a few metres into the woods and stand facing the German positions in the trees on the other side of the road. This track was the axis of advance for A Company. The commanding officer's plan was that it would break through across the Dreijenseweg to capture the Lichtenbeek feature just 500 metres beyond the road. B Company would then move on to reinforce the position followed by C Company and the rest of the battalion thereby providing a firm position upon which the balance of the Brigade's advance to the next feature, called Koepel, and about 1,000 metres further on, would be based. From here it would launch itself onto its objectives in the north of Arnhem some three kilometres yet further on.

The company advanced at 8.30 am with one platoon out in front. The basic theory was that the lead platoon would run into any enemy and set about fighting hard to dominate the area; a process known as 'winning the fire fight'. Whilst the fire of the lead platoon was suppressing the enemy one or both of the other two platoons, depending on the size of the opposition, would seek to carry out a flanking attack.

Let us assume that the company was at reasonable strength, and therefore the forward platoon would be about thirty strong, with a section of eight either side of the track and the third section in reserve. Given the five metres between each man they had learnt in training, but accepting that woods and proximity to the enemy drive men closer together, we can presume a section frontage of about thirty metres on either side of the track. As they approached the road they came under fire from the enemy to their front, and from two half-tracks from just where your car is parked. Major John Pott had little choice but to try and outflank the Germans to the left, avoiding the open ground and half-tracks to his right. However, he was at some disadvantage. Back on the DZ his No 3 platoon had been left behind to guard prisoners and

80

the wounded, and had been substituted by a platoon composed of Glider Pilots. This was a normal use of Glider Pilots in the British Army, for they were all trained as infantry and could give a good account of themselves. However, they had not worked previously with the company and had not been trained in its drills and procedures. Quite why they could not have guarded the prisoners and No 3 Platoon been left in its proper place does not appear ever to have been explained.

Major Pott had only the briefest time to give his orders, calling to the lead platoon by the road where you are standing to be the 'fire platoon.' This gave them the role of keeping up an intense fire on the enemy positions to permit a left-flanking attack by the rest of the company. Ordering 4 Platoon and the Glider Pilots to go 'left flanking' they attacked, which would have put 4 Platoon some fifty to 100 metres away from you, with a frontage of some sixty to eighty metres. This is a considerable distance in woodland, and John Pott records that the Glider Pilot platoon had not appeared, having been held up in more open ground to the left. They would have been some distance away from where you now are, and possibly exposed to the open ground where the 10th Battalion battle was fought, the southern edge of which is 400 metres away.

The officer commanding 5 Platoon was killed, shortly followed by his counterpart in 4 Platoon, to be followed by the second-in-command of the Glider Pilot platoon, whilst the Glider Pilot platoon commander was wounded. Captain Terry Rogers, who had brought up a 6-pounder and tried to take on the armoured vehicles with it, was fatally wounded. Major Pott, determined to make every effort to speed the path to assist his brother-in-law, John Frost, at the Bridge, drove through the enemy with very few men left. He paused at one stage to pray, standing in the open, over some of his worst wounded soldiers before pressing on.

However, although he got to the objective it was with only six men. Out of ammunition and hit in the thigh and hand there was nothing he could do when, at about 2.30 pm, his position was taken by a German platoon whose commander remarked in perfect English: 'Sorry we can't see to you now, but your chaps will be back soon anyway.' He was to lay there for a long time, eventually being taken prisoner, the only officer of A Company to survive the battle.

As the A Company battle was going on the CO ordered Major John Waddy's B Company, at about 9.00 am, to attack on the same alignment, citing as his reasons the need to drive on and the fact that the opposition appeared to be limited to snipers. Given the volume of fire that was churning up the ground, smashing through the trees and exploding overhead just where you are standing it remains difficult to understand how he formed this conclusion. On his way to form up for his assault Major Waddy passed an entire platoon headquarters from A Company lying dead on the track.

However, Major Waddy took his company into the assault on a two-platoon frontage. They came under intense fire, much of which was from 20mm cannon. The important thing about 20mm ammunition is that it is the smallest round into which high explosive can be filled and for which a fuze could be made. Consequently, when it hit the target it detonated. If the target was a man, he exploded. If it was a tree the shards of metal from the detonating round and splinters from the tree flew everywhere, causing terrible injuries. If the hit was high on the tree then the effect was similar to an airburst, which meant that men lying down trying to take cover from direct fire were exposed to the risk of wounding from above. It was a nightmare. Private Ron Atkinson was in the thick of it all:

'We heard the clatter of tank tracks to our front and flank using the narrow paths among the trees. They let off everything they had at us: small arms, armour-piercing shells, high explosive, the lot. We advanced at the double, since it was pointless waiting to be massacred. Our section sergeant was hit, and while assisting to place him on a stretcher I was hit at the back of the neck by a tree-burst. My hands and tunic sleeves were covered with blood.[2]*'*

Major John Waddy's description of events happening all around where you are standing is equally graphic:

'German armoured vehicles were moving along the Dreijensche (sic) *Weg firing madly at my company. A twin-barreled 20mm anti-aircraft gun on the road opened up, firing high-explosive shells that burst in the trees and flung out deadly splinters. Several men crawling on the ground were killed or wounded. As both leading platoons were held up I crept forward with some soldiers to knock the gun out. We got within ten paces... the man on my right was about to throw a phosphorus grenade when he was drilled through the head by a man sitting in a tree above the gun. Instead of the German* Schmeisser *I normally carried on this morning I had only a pistol. I missed with my first shots, and then he hit me. I collapsed and started to crawl out. Our mortars were now firing on the road. A figure burst through the bushes saying: "come on, sir, let's get you out of here." It was Ben Diedricks, a 6'4" Rhodesian miner. By then the battalion attack was stalled.*[3]*'*

An example of a German 20mm anti-aircraft gun mounted on a halftrack.

With A and B Companies destroyed, Lieutenant Colonel des Voeux sought to recover something from the situation by pulling together HQ and Support Companies into a fighting element under Major Michael Page. However, their attempt, at around 10.30 am, to break through was beaten back, with considerable loss.

In the early afternoon the battalion was withdrawn as part of the Brigade withdrawal back to Wolfheze, with only C Company left as a cohesive fighting sub-unit. The move was made at the same time as 10th Battalion and marked the end of any attempt to reach the Bridge in Arnhem. As they withdrew they could see supply aircraft dropping their loads on areas which it was planned they would have occupied beyond the Dreijenseweg, but which the Germans still held.

Before you leave, thinking perhaps that the 4 Brigade task had been hopeless and that they had no chance of ever really reaching their objectives, it is worth calling to mind SS-*Sturmmann* Alfred Ziegler. He was standing next to his battlegroup commander, SS-*Hauptsturmführer* Bruhns, after the early attacks by the two British battalions when his officer confided: 'if we do not get any reinforcement soon we shall have to withdraw when the next attack comes';[4] and this despite German superiority in men and weapons.

The German position was showing the first signs of cracking when their reinforcements arrived in the shape of a company of self-propelled anti-aircraft artillery, with the addition of a battalion of twin and quadruple 20mm anti-aircraft guns mounted on half-tracks which just appeared out of the blue. The firepower of these additions was phenomenal, and they turned the tide. But be in no doubt, they were hard and resourceful men those British paratroopers and had they not been completely outgunned, and then only at the last minute by men who themselves were top grade soldiers, they would have prevailed.

Return to your car and drive down the hill towards the railway bridge. Immediately before it there is a left turn signed to the **Airborne Cemetery**. **Turn down here** and stop on the right as soon as it is safe and convenient to do so. Leave your car, return to the Dreijenseweg, cross the road and stand at the entrance to Johannahoeveweg where you can look due south down Stationsweg on the other side of the bridge and due north up Dreijenseweg. We are here at the scene of an ambush involving 2nd Parachute Platoon, 250 Airborne Light Company RASC. Just where you are standing was a signal keeper's house during the war.

The company's role was to supply ammunition fuel and food to each of the Brigades, and it had one platoon for each of the three brigades. The balance of the company, including the company commander, was in the Seaborne Echelon; that element of the Division comprising some 2,200 logistic and administrative vehicles and 1,100 men that could not be airdropped or airlanded for one reason or another and was making its way up the corridor behind the XXX Corps' thrust. They would only ever get as far as Nijmegen.

The Divisional Administrative Area (DAA) in which two of the platoons were located was on the triangle of land on the other side of Utrechtseweg from the Hartenstein Hotel. If you look along Stationsweg you will remember that the Hartenstein is to the right of the crossroads at the bottom of the road and in your mind's eye should be able to position their location, about 800 metres south-west of where

The Royal Army Service Corps.

you are standing. The third platoon was already in Arnhem at the Bridge with those elements of 1st Parachute Brigade that had made it that far.

You will remember that as the soldiers of 156 Parachute Battalion were withdrawing in mid-afternoon on 19 September they reported seeing re-supply flights overhead. These aircraft were seeking to drop onto the open ground beyond the Dreijenseweg, about a kilometre north-east of your present position, although a number of parachutes with supplies landed around where you are

84

standing and further up the Dreijenseweg. Down in the DAA these drops could be seen, and Captain Desmond Kavanagh of the RASC, commanding 2nd Parachute Platoon, was sent out to collect in what he could.

Each RASC platoon had five jeeps, each capable of towing two trailers. There are differing accounts of how many jeeps were in Kavanagh's party, anywhere between three and five. However, Driver Ron Pearce probably clarifies the matter in his description of what happened:

> 'Captain Kavanagh said there were two jobs, one lot to go to recce the DZ to look for supplies, and one lot with shells to the bridge. He disappeared with three jeeps. The team that went for the bridge took one jeep with two trailers and got as far as the St Elisabeth Hospital. Here we were stopped by an officer who asked what we were doing. On hearing he told us we should go back, we wouldn't get 300 yards.'

Corporal Burnham Blaxley indicates, however, that there may have been more jeeps:

> 'Captain Kavanagh detailed me to prepare my section for immediate departure to pick up these newly dropped supplies. On this occasion I decided to take only one trailer per jeep; this would provide extra mobility. I left one man, Driver Stevens, to guard the remaining trailers. Captain Kavanagh occupied Jeep Number One, driven by Driver Thomas. I followed in Jeep Number Two driven, I believe, by Driver Doherty. The remaining jeeps took up position behind me, supervised by Lance Corporal J Syme. Sergeant McDowell was with the Platoon Scout Section who spread themselves out among the convoy.'

Corporal Burnham Blaxley RASC.
Collection F R Steer

Looking down Stationsweg you would have seen the small convoy racing up the road towards where you are standing at around 3.00 pm. Paddy Kavanagh and his men headed towards the supply dropping zones, passing as they did so a burning Bren carrier with the crew all dead around

An example of a British Bren gun carrier and crew.

it. Given this gruesome sight, and the noise from the battle that had been going on most of the day just beyond the bridge they were approaching, some caution might have been appropriate. Captain Kavanagh, however, was not a cautious officer and he led his jeeps, at speed, straight across the bridge. In those days the bridge was very much more of a 'hump-backed' construction than is the case with the current structure. Consequently, their view of the ground beyond it was limited.

It was just a few metres away from you, opposite the second house

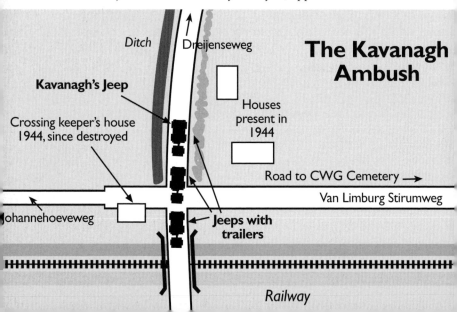

The Kavanagh Ambush

Ditch

Dreijenseweg

Kavanagh's Jeep

Houses present in 1944

Crossing keeper's house 1944, since destroyed

Road to CWG Cemetery →

Van Limburg Stirumweg

Johannehoeveweg

Jeeps with trailers

Railway

The ambush scene, taken by a German photographer shortly afterwards and after the vehicles had been cleared away. Bundersarchiv Bild 101 1/2KBK 771/18

The ambush scene as it is today looking south. Courtesy Drs Robert P G A Voskuil

Railway bridge

Ditch

Direction of Kavanagh's route

on the right up Dreijenseweg, that a German gun further up the road stopped the lead Jeep with a shell through the front. Up went the bonnet; the vehicles behind were going at such a rate they telescoped into each other and men leapt out to the left and right. Captain Kavanagh went to the left into the ditch you can see running beside the road, leaving his dead driver in the Jeep. Driver Ken Clarke with his Bren gun leapt from the trailer of the second vehicle and went down into the ditch just near where you are standing. He began at once to fire his gun underneath the jeep and trailer at Germans in the houses and gardens opposite. Meanwhile, Burnham Blaxley was otherwise engaged on the right of the road:

Captain Desmond Kavanaç RASC. Collection F R Steer

> *'I dived from the jeep into a hedge and then into a garden where two of our men, both severely wounded, were already taking cover. They were Percy Batsford and Wilfred Bennet, who later died of his wounds and is buried in an unknown grave.'*

Paddy Kavanagh, realising his position was untenable, knew the only escape route lay back over the railway near the bridge they had just crossed. He decided on bold course of action, involving Ken Clarke and his Bren gun:

> *'He exchanged his Sten for my Bren and said: "When I stand up you all run back over the bridge." This he did, standing in the road and obviously diverting attention to himself.'*

Of course, having taken Ken Clarke's Bren gun, Desmond Kavanagh

The .303 Bren gun. It weighed 22.5lb with a rate of fire of up to 500 rounds per minute from a 30 round box magazine.

The 9mm Sten machine gun. It was cheap to produce and with a 32 round box magazine, was a useful close-quarter weapon. The airborne version shown here was a much prized capture by the SS, who preferred it to the Schmeisser as it was much easier to fire from the prone position.

had his pouches full of Sten magazines with their 9mm ammunition. Ken now had a Sten gun with his pouches stuffed with Bren magazines containing .303-inch ammunition. In making the change Paddy Kavanagh had limited both men's firepower to only the thirty rounds or so they each had in the magazine on their weapon.

Corporal Dennis Cutting remembers the officer shouting to Sergeant McDowell to get them out, referring to his men. As they were running back Ken Clarke was ordered to cover the withdrawal with his newly acquired Sten gun, and he did so from the corner of the railway bridge right where you are standing. He was the last to leave as the others ran down the embankment to the railway, and was quite sure he knew at that stage that his Captain had been killed. After a short pause to regain their breath, they made their way up the other side of the embankment and sought to escape back to the DAA, although it was not easy, as Corporal Dennis Cutting explained:

Driver Ken Clarke RASC.
Collection F R Steer

'Three of us threw ourselves onto the barbed wire and the others ran across our bodies and pulled us off. We got into a row of houses and were arguing which way was best to go, because the Germans were all over the place. Across the road a door opened and this huge chap, skinny as a rake, appeared with a little girl. He could not speak English, but she

Corporal Dennis Cutting (left) RASC. Collection F R Steer

could, and said she would lead us out. She went down the road and beckoned us one by one.'

As for Burnham Blaxley, he was taken prisoner:

'I defended myself and my wounded until, whilst changing my magazine, I was ordered to put down my weapon and stand up. Looking over my shoulder I saw a German lieutenant speaking excellent English and aiming a long barreled Luger directly at me. I had no choice but to obey. I was instructed to find a jeep that worked which, eventually, I did and put my two wounded in it. The German officer put his wounded in alongside and, accompanied by the officer, I drove the jeep back behind German lines. It was then I saw the German armoured vehicles and self-propelled guns and realised there was no hope whatsoever of any recovery being made with our inadequate resources. We were sitting ducks.'

Prior to moving off with his wounded, and whilst searching for a useable jeep, Burnham saw the body of Desmond Kavanagh propped up by the bonnet of the first vehicle, showing all the signs of having slithered down by his jeep. His weapon was on the ground beside him. Burnham was in for another shock just a few minutes later. Whilst helping one of the wounded to the only useable jeep left in the small column he was forced by a 6-inch mortar barrage directed onto the road itself to take cover in a German slit trench, with Germans still in it. Initial concerns at the possible implications of this were soon

The Air Despatch memorial. Behind, in the field, is where Harry Simmonds' load landed.

dispelled when the Germans burst into laughter at the situation in which they all found themselves.

Back in the Seaborne Echelon Lt R G Adams RASC commanded one of the platoons in 250 Airborne Light Company. He went on in later life to write his masterpiece, *Watership Down*, basing it on the battle in Oosterbeek and with many of the characters loosely drawn from men in the company. Only two of the characters were directly based on individuals, and Desmond Kavanagh was Bigwig.

Return to your car and **proceed to the cemetery**. This may be the time when you decide to make your visit, but however you choose to do so you should, at some stage, drive on past the cemetery entrance about 200 metres to the Air Despatch Memorial and park. Here you can look across the fields behind the memorial at the Dreijenseweg and see it from the German perspective; and see just how much space they had to manoeuvre and re-deploy to meet any 4 Brigade threat.

Soldiers of the RASC rig parachutes to panniers ready for loading onto a Dakota or a Stirling bomber. TAYLOR LIBRARY

Driver Harry Simmonds RASC.
Collection F R Steer

The Air Despatch memorial commemorates the names of seventy-nine air despatchers who died attempting to deliver re-supply by air to the men of Arnhem. Soldiers of the RASC, they were responsible for packing the panniers and containers containing supplies, rigging them for parachuting, loading them onto the aircraft and then despatching them over the dropping zone. If you look into the field behind the memorial it was here that Driver Harry Simmonds was to help despatch a load of sixteen panniers from a Dakota on what was to be his only trip over Holland.

'The manifest for the drop showed compo in all panniers, but when we got to the airfield we were switched to another aircraft carrying plastic explosive and petrol. Approaching the DZ there was a great bang and a tracer came through the fuselage and jammed in one of the rollers where it burnt itself out. Our crew commander, a dour Yorkshireman, stood in the doorway and shouted: "Bloody 'ell, there's a hell of a battle going on down there." Then a tracer bullet came through the open door. "Bloody cheek, they're shooting at us"!'

The battle they were witnessing was the final stage of the 4th Parachute Brigade action, with the Germans by this time chasing the withdrawing paratroopers. This would have allowed the anti-aircraft guns and other heavy weapons in Spindler's force to bring all their weight to bear on the slow-moving re-supply aircraft. Harry's load fell among the Germans in the field just behind the memorial, and perhaps we might wonder if it was the sight of those parachutes, among others, that attracted Desmond Kavanagh's fatal expedition to this area.

There are many stories of courage and devotion to duty by air despatchers and RAF aircrew over Arnhem; many more than can be properly told in this short book. There have been many epitaphs, but probably Major General Urquhart, writing of the demise of Dakota KG-374 whose pilot, Flight Lieutenant David Lord, was to be one of the Arnhem VCs, sums them all:

'One Dakota was hit by flak, and the starboard wing set on fire. Yet it came on, descending to 900 feet. It seemed that every anti-aircraft gun in the vicinity was sighted on the crippled aircraft. With its starboard engine blazing, it came through to the dropping zone. At the end of the run the Dakota turned and made a second run to drop the remaining supplies. From foxholes and slit trenches and from the restricted spaces to which we were trying to attract the pilots; from blasted buildings and ditches and emplacements of rubble and earth, the eyes of hundreds and probably thousands of careworn soldiers gazed upwards through the battle haze. We were spellbound and speechless, and I dare say there is not a survivor of Arnhem who will ever forget, or want to forget, the courage we were privileged to witness in those terrible eight minutes.[5]'

Flight Lieutenant David S. A. Lord DFC.

There were others who saw what happened to Lord's aircraft. Lance Corporal C Marshall RASC of 63 Airborne Composite Company RASC had friends in the air despatch crew on the aircraft:

'Approaching the Dutch border Phil Nixon's plane was hit and the starboard engine was out of action. His Dakota, on my port side, lost altitude and was lost to my view as it veered underneath us. I was hoping he would bale out, but he was not a trained parachutist. Either that, or he and the flight crew were adamant in attempting their despatching. Whatever it was, they were forced to make a second pass over the DZ and this allowed Phil to despatch his load just before the "Dak" exploded. The pilot, Flight Lieutenant Lord, received the VC for his bravery. Whether Phil's bravery was cited for "sticking to his guns" I'll never know. His wife had recently given birth to Brenda who I believe was six weeks old. I cannot say whether Phil had seen her before he was killed.

Here, men in Oosterbeek unpack one of the wicker panniers. TAYLOR LIBRARY

Fifty years later, at a lunch with the Princess Royal in Wellington Barracks, my eyes met another pair across the room. "You're Mickey Marshall, aren't you; my Dad's best friend." She was the spitting image of Phil.'

Harry Simmonds was lucky. Despite the attentions of the German flak units, and just about anyone else who could fire a weapon skywards, his aircraft completed its mission and returned safely to base. Others were not so fortunate. Corporal Jack Sales was a crew commander in 253 Company. He cannot remember all the details or dates for his drops. Sticking in his mind, however, was the young despatcher who made the mistake of wearing his parachute whilst despatching and was caught up by a disappearing pannier and was carried to his death. Air despatchers had a parachute available in the aircraft, which was known as an observers' 'chute, and was worn on the chest and not the back. Wearing them during despatching could be dangerous, as witness Corporal Sales' example, and was not normally encouraged.

One of Harry Simmonds' friends was killed that day – Harry tells the story:

'Norman Enderby was on the same mission as me, on the same day. He had made the drop and was returning to the coast when they were hit. He was married, and his wife was pregnant with triplets. He has no known grave.'

Norman's aircraft, a Stirling, was hit by flak over enemy-held territory, and crashed in the municipality of Aardenburg, diving nose first into the ground. It was completely compressed, and when the wreckage was recovered in 1945 it was impossible to identify any of the occupants.

There was one survivor from Lord's aircraft, the navigator, Flight Lieutenant H J King RAF. In describing his feelings about the air despatchers from his own aircraft he summed them all:

'These men were not volunteers like aircrew. They received no flying pay, yet were, without doubt, superb in their fulfillment of duty ...'

This is a proud heritage, carried today in the modern British Army by 47 Air Despatch Squadron of the Royal Logistic Corps.

Returning to your car drive back to the scene of Desmond Kavanagh's ambush, **turn left** over the bridge and then **immediately right** into Nico Bovenweg whereupon you should try to **stop on the right** of the road. You will see that you are on a kind of roundabout arrangement of roads and you will shortly be taking the second right

The 'White House', Hotel Dreijeroord. Courtesy Drs Robert P G A Voskuil

down Graaf van Rechterenweg before returning later to proceed along Nico Bovenweg. The purpose of this short halt is to give you a moment to reflect on the areas of fighting you have just visited and the fact that running down Stationsweg on this side of the road was what would become the front line of the eastern edge of the Oosterbeek 'Thumb'. You may remember when you drove up Stationsweg to visit this area you passed the houses that were occupied by 156 Parachute Battalion. In fact, all that was left by then was mainly C Company, finishing up just a few hundred metres from its battle in the woods, a little way off to the north of where you are parked, having got there via a withdrawal to the area of Wolfheze and yet another battle in the woods, of which more later.

Drive into Graaf van Rechterenweg and follow it just a few metres to its **junction** with Van Dedemweg on the left.

On the south-west corner of this junction stands a hotel, the Dreijeroord. Every member of the KOSB, knows this, from its colour, as the 'White House', for this was the area of the perimeter they eventually occupied and defended. This was the northernmost part of the 'thumb'. And the defensive posture of the KOSB was itself thumb-shaped. Walk or drive the few metres to the next junction, with Karel van Gelderlaan, and you are where C Company held the western edge

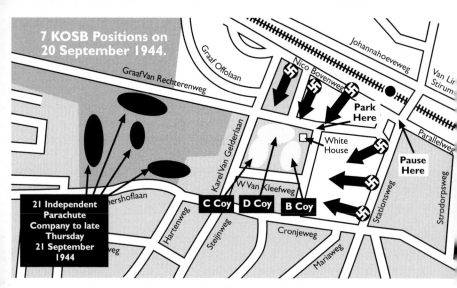

7 KOSB Positions on 20 September 1944.

Graaf Offolaan

GraafVan Rechterenweg

Johannahoeveweg

Nico Bovenweg

Van Lir Stirum

Park Here

Karel Van Gelderlaan

White House

Parallelweg

W Van Kleefweg

Pause Here

Strodorpsweg

21 Independent Parachute Company to late Thursday 21 September 1944

...ershoflaan

C Coy **D Coy** **B Coy**

Hartenweg

Steijnweg

Cronjeweg

Stationsweg

...weg

Mariaweg

of the battalion area down Karel van Gelderlaan, and part of the northern and southern boundaries.

By 20 September, when this area was occupied by the KOSB, C Company was the strongest left in the battalion. D Company held the remainder of the northern end, along which you have just walked from the hotel; its area of responsibility included the hotel itself, which

Men of 1 Border manning a 6-pounder anti-tank gun on the western perimeter. The gun's name 'Gallipoli' can be seen on the shield. TAYLOR LIBRARY

A Vickers machine-gun team keeping watch. Although the gun was accurate and reliable, the major problem was a lack of ammunition as re-supply drops were falling into enemy hands.
TAYLOR LIBRARY

dominated the area. B Company, very much its remnants with three-quarters having been taken prisoner near Wolfheze, and with a party of Glider Pilots from F Squadron under command, held the remainder of the southern edge of the area along Cronjéweg. A Company was no more, having been taken prisoner on 19 and 20 September.

They were in a reasonable position for a battalion so badly battered. They had five of their eight anti-tank guns left, and with them were able to cover every road. The remaining 3″-mortars they pooled centrally, and what Vickers medium machine-guns there were the CO placed with D Company. They were, however, somewhat exposed, as their nearest friendly unit was the Reconnaissance Squadron on Stationsweg and there was a gap of 200 metres on the left before reaching the 21st Independent Parachute Company.

This was an area of terrible fighting. Just to the north was the

German snipers caused numerous casualties. Here an example from elsewhere shows their sniper rifle and camouflage.

railway embankment across which Germans could easily approach and in cover. Initially, the KOSB covered the area, including the gaps with flanking units, with standing patrols, but as their casualties grew worse and worse this became impossible. They suffered mortaring and artillery fire, some of the latter directly from marauding self-propelled guns; they were sniped at constantly from the trees and from buildings occupied by the Germans; and the machine-gun fire seemed never ending. However, the KOSB anti-tank gunners gave a good account of themselves until their ammunition ran out, PIATs were found to be useful in dislodging snipers, the mortars and machine-guns were well used, and some aggressive patrolling meant that the Germans did not have an easy time of it, even though they were forcing the KOSB constantly to shorten their line. Lieutenant Erskine Carter, a Canadian officer on loan to the KOSB, was involved in one particular incident:

'From the vicinity of the White House numerous heavy calibre machine-guns chattered supporting fire and more than a hundred shouting SS troopers charged over the forty yards towards our positions. Our front position casualties were heavy and we fell back fifty yards, but the Vickers gunners stuck to their guns. Reorganised by the Colonel, who ran ahead tossing grenades and supported by our machine guns, whose devastating fire kept the Jerry machine-gun replies to a minimum, we fixed bayonets and went after the

Hun. It was a costly business, enemy bullets ripped around us, but still we pressed on. After covering about half the distance to the enemy, the Colonel ordered us to the ground and the Vickers swept the woods to our front. Many German soldiers elected to stay in their trenches and fight to the end and their trenches were filled with dead Germans. Soon the whole area, which we had to give up at various stages in the previous twelve hours, was in our hands. We quickly consolidated and then we attended to our wounded...there were about fifteen dead and many more wounded. Some of our bravest had died leading the charge.[6']

It is perhaps worth remembering that 7 KOSB was a Territorial Army battalion, the only one at Arnhem, and the CO had been considered too old to command a regular battalion.

Drive **back the way you came**, and **turn left** down Nico Bovenweg. Driving along beside the railway gives you a feel for the area, on your left and right, through which the Germans had to make their way in order to assault the KOSB and those other units in the northern part of the perimeter. With the trip meter by now on **5.8 miles/9.3 kilometers** you will be at a junction on your left with Valkenburglaan; and it is also signed as part of the marked cycle route around the battlefield. Proceed **down Valkenburglaan to 6.4 miles/10.3 kilometers** on the trip meter and **turn right into Sportlaan**, where you should **park** as soon as you safely can. Leave the car and then **carry on, walking, along Valkenburglaan** to a marker post about fifty metres further on. You are now by what is known by some as the '**4 Brigade Hole**' and by others as the '**Hollow**'.

Walk **along the track** which heads west alongside the edge of the wood in which is the large dip in the ground in which the remnants of 4 Brigade spent a large part of 20 September 1944. Look, as you do, at the trees: much smaller in 1944 they still bear the scars of the battle that took place here. **Remain on the track** or **make your way down into the dip**. If you face west, along the line of the track, Bredelaan is

The '4 Brigade Hole' or 'Hollow'. Courtesy Drs Robert P G A Voskuil

about 1,000 metres away, and you will remember having parked your car in it on the first tour. Early on the morning of 20 September the remnants of 4th Parachute Brigade, comprising the HQ and what was left of 156 and 10th Battalions, were moving down Bredelaan with a view to getting to Utrechtseweg and making their way eastwards into the perimeter. They were hit by Germans positioned on the junction of Utrechtseweg and Bredelaan and had to abandon that idea. Moving back the way they had come for a short distance, Brigadier Hackett ordered 10th Parachute Battalion to make its own way into the perimeter, taking a more northerly route, whilst he went with 156 Battalion further to the south. Standing where you are, and facing north back the way you came along Valkenburglaan, the 10th Battalion would have crossed, left to right, some two-thirds of the way back to the railway line and entered the perimeter in the area occupied by 21 Independent Parachute Company, half of 4 Parachute Squadron RE and some Glider Pilots. They were in by about 1.00 pm on 20 September, and the Commanding Officer reported to Major General Urquhart on his arrival, with just 60 men from the battalion that had left England complete two days earlier.

Brigadier Hackett's group were forced by German infantry armed with machine-guns to take cover in the 'hole'. There were a few German soldiers in it when the paratroopers arrived, but they were all quickly killed or made prisoner. By now Brigadier Hackett's direct command, which had been some 2,500 men only three days earlier, was

German SS captured near Wolfheze. Sgt Joe Kitchener of the Glider Pilot Regiment (arrowed) is one of their guards. Taylor Library

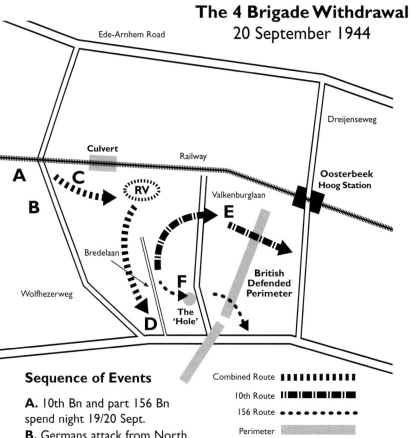

The 4 Brigade Withdrawal
20 September 1944

Ede-Arnhem Road

Dreijenseweg

Culvert

Railway

A

C

RV

Valkenburglaan

B

Oosterbeek
Hoog Station

E

Bredelaan

British
Defended
Perimeter

Wolfhezerweg

F

The
'Hole'

D

Sequence of Events

Combined Route

10th Route

156 Route

Perimeter

A. 10th Bn and part 156 Bn
spend night 19/20 Sept.
B. Germans attack from North,
156 Bn suffers heavily.
C. 10th Bn joins main bde group,
which includes 156 Bn from
overnight position.
D. Morning of 20 Sept, main
group hits opposition and splits.

E. 10th Bn into perimeter by
13.30
F. Bde HQ and 156 Bn in hollow
(4th Bde Hole) all afternoon and
then break out in the evening.

down to 150; and all in one large hole in the ground. Major Geoffrey
Powell, C Company Commander, was now commanding 156
Parachute Battalion, Lieutenant Colonel des Voeux having been killed
earlier on the way to the 'hole'.

The Germans were determined not to let the paratroopers escape
and maintained an intense fire on them. Several hours after they had
arrived, and just as darkness began to approach, Brigadier Hackett
decided he would have to break out. The situation was desperate, and
half of the 150 had been killed or wounded.

View of the open area east of 'Hackett's Hollow', looking south-east in the direction of the Sonnenburg, visible in the distance. A Company 1 Border was in trenches in the centre of the picture and had been since 19 September. Courtesy Drs Robert P G A Voskuil

Return now to the marker post, stand facing Valkenburglaan at right angles and then turn about 20 degrees right. You are now facing Sonnenberg; the area on the perimeter's edge occupied by A Company the Border Regiment that had taken up the position in the afternoon of 19 September 1944.

In a single body, screaming like banshees, Brigadier Hackett led his remaining men in a charge 300 metres to get into the British position. As they stopped, exhausted, in the relative safety of the perimeter, a Border Regiment captain in whose area they halted invited Geoffrey Powell to 'take away this filthy lot before they contaminate my men!'[7]

The consolidated strength of 4th Parachute Brigade that evening, including what was left of 11th Battalion, was probably no more than 500 men. The Brigade was given the responsibility for defending the eastern side of the perimeter – nearest to Arnhem.

As you **drive back you might go to the car park** by the Schoonoord Restaurant at the Oosterbeek crossroads. Between this car park and the Hartenstein there is a large, detached house and then there is the church, where the coaches park. Brigadier Hackett's HQ was in a house very similar to the first one, but on the site next to the church which is a post-war construction. Time now for refreshment, before the next tour.

[1] From *Off At Last* by Robert Sigmond, 1997.
[2] From *Salute To The Steadfast – From Delhi To Arnhem With 151/156 Parachute Battalion'* by Harry Bankhead, Ramsay Press, 1999.
[3] *ibid*
[4] From *It Never Snows in September* by Robert J Kershaw, The Crowood Press, 1990.
[5] From *Arnhem* by Major General R E Urquhart CB DSO, Cassel, 1958.
[6] From *Off At Last* by Robert Sigmond, 1997.
[7] From *Salute To The Steadfast* by Harry Bankhead, Ramsay Press, 1999.

Chapter Four

A WALK IN THE PERIMETER

Duration – 90 minutes on foot

No visit to Oosterbeek is complete without a walk around key parts of the perimeter within a radius of a few hundred metres of the Airborne Museum 'Hartenstein'. **Begin with a stroll down Pietersbergseweg** past the Schoonoord towards the right hand bend you will be able to see about 200 metres ahead. There you will find the Huize de Tafelberg. It was a hotel prior to the battle and was the actual location of Model's HQ. It was the building he used personally, although he had staff also working in the Hartenstein; not surprising given the size of an Army Group HQ. During the battle, de Tafelberg was used as a medical installation. In its current, modern-day form it retains the façade, but is now used for other purposes.

Field Ambulances were established to provide medical support to formations on operations. These were company sized units, and for 1st Airborne Division there was one per brigade; each with a strength of about 180 men. A wounded soldier would first be treated with immediate first aid in his Company Aid Post, before moving to the Regimental Aid Post, or RAP, at battalion level. Here he would see his

Wounded soldiers receive medical treatment in 9 Duitsekampweg in Wolfheze. Taylor Library

De Tafelberg in 1945. Courtesy Drs Robert P G A Voskuil

De Tafelberg in 2001.

first doctor, but treatment would be limited to preparation for evacuation to the Field Ambulance. Again, treatment here was limited, with surgery normally only being undertaken as a life-saving measure. Full treatment would await arrival at the next level of medical support: a field hospital some way behind the front. As a rule, casualties should be with a surgeon within six hours of wounding in order to preclude the onset of additional complications, of which gangrene was one.

However, cut off from external support Airborne or Airlanding Field Ambulances each brought with them two surgical teams capable of carrying out quite extensive surgical procedures. This allowed them to substitute, as best they could, for the facilities that would normally be provided by the next level of medical support, unavailable to airborne soldiers until they had linked with ground troops. The Schoonoord

With the ever increasing flow of casualties, hotel cellars and houses were used as first aid posts. Here a wounded soldier is being stretchered into the house in 9 Duitsekampweg, Wolfheze, for treatment. TAYLOR LIBRARY

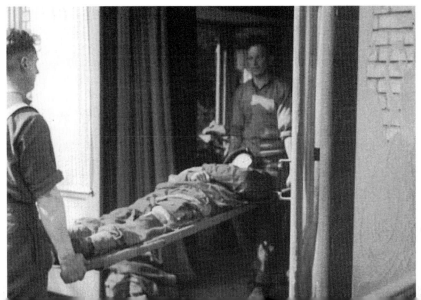

The Schoonoord Hotel in 1945, just the shell remaining after a V weapon strike. Courtesy Drs Robert P G A Voskuil

was occupied by 181 Airlanding Field Ambulance, supporting the Airlanding Brigade. Its two surgical teams were located in de Tafelberg.

You will remember from the previous tour that this road was the front line for both sides; and, unusually, medical units were right in the front line. Consequently, Germans visited them from time to time and, once the enemy had become used to the fact that they were medical units, the relationship between both sides inside the Schoonoord and de Tafelberg, whilst never easy, permitted a degree of tolerant cohabitation. Private Roland Atkinson of 156 Parachute Battalion described a visit by a German officer who appeared not at all pleased with what he found, despite assurances from a British doctor that German wounded were being treated as well as their British counterparts, and were upstairs. The German officer spent thirty minutes upstairs and came down:

> '...with a huge smile on his face, and walked down the lines of the British Para's giving each a Woodbine cigarette. He shook hands with the doctor, clicked his heels together, disappeared into his tank and rumbled back down the road towards Arnhem.'[1']

The Schoonoord Restaurant 2001, on the right of the picture, much smaller and with offices and shops where its full frontage was in 1944. The petrol station is at the extreme left of the picture.

Some of the visits, however, were not quite so pleasant, as Private Tom Bannister of 181 A/L Field Ambulance reported:

> *The SS marched all the orderlies outside and lined us up with hands on heads near the garage we were using as a mortuary. It looked as though that was it. I was standing next to a chap named Stan Biggs, and he looked across to me, grinned and said "Well, there is one thing, Tom, they won't have far to carry us".[2]*

Fortunately, the implied threat was never carried out.

Walk back up from de Tafelberg and **turn right at the crossroads**, towards Arnhem. You are walking along the front of the Schoonoord, which in 1944 was a very much larger hotel than the restaurant it is today. It extended all the way to the petrol station some fifty metres down the road; a petrol station earmarked by the logisticians in Divisional HQ to provide eight gallons of fuel per vehicle per day – a purpose for which it was never really used. On the opposite corner of the crossroads was a hotel called the Vreewijk where additional patient care was undertaken by medical staff of 181 Field Ambulance. You can still see the name above the main door of the building, although it is now used as offices.

The Germans took possession of the Schoonoord on the morning of Wednesday 20 September following an exchange of fire with a self-propelled gun which damaged the building, killed a number of people and wounded yet again others who had already suffered wounds. A V weapon eventually destroyed the Schoonoord during the winter of

The Vreewijk Hotel taken shortly before the war. Courtesy Drs Robert P G A Voskuil

Annastraat. No.2

1944, and the site now houses the restaurant and café and a number of offices and shops.

Proceed down the road to the **first turning on your right**, called Annastraat. You have just walked the length of the so-called '10 Para Finger', a salient held by the 10th Battalion from its arrival in the perimeter on the afternoon of Wednesday 20 September.

The 10th Battalion were relieved by the relocation of 21 Independent Parachute Company from the north-east edge of the perimeter very early on the morning of Saturday 23 September, whereupon the battalion, by now down to some thirty men, was withdrawn into 'reserve'. The salient extended two rows of houses deep, back from the main road.

When the 10th Battalion moved into position on the Wednesday they had to skirt around the Germans in the Schoonoord in order to occupy the houses, which they had to wrest from the grasp of SS infantry who were already in residence. Accounts of just how many buildings they occupied vary between eight and four. The 10th Battalion having gained its foothold, the Germans in the Schoonoord left during the Wednesday night.

Proceed down Annastraat just a few metres and you will see on your left a detached family home, No 2 – the first house.

This was as far forward as the salient reached. The German attacks were fierce, and the cellar of the house was used to hold wounded. These included Lieutenant Colonel Smyth, who had already sustained injury during the Battalion's earlier adventures. On Thursday 21 September he was wounded again, this time mortally, when a German soldier threw a hand grenade into the cellar. His injuries paralysed him and he was to die several weeks later in hospital. Among the civilians in the cellar was Mrs Bertje Voskuil. She would have been killed or seriously wounded by the grenade had not Private Albert Willingham stood in the way. Taking the full force of the blast he fell across her, bleeding profusely and quite dead. Reports of the state of the cellar speak of it swimming in blood, and it was clearly not a pleasant place to be. Eventually, the surviving military occupants were made prisoner, but despite having taken the building the Germans were unable to gain great advantage from the position.

From Annastraat **walk back to the main road and turn right towards Arnhem**. A few metres along is another turning to the right: Lukassenpad. Go down here just fifty metres and view the back of No 2 Annastraat. This gives you an 'enemy's eye' feel for the approach to the British perimeter and the small alleyway is very much as it looked in 1944 with just a couple of buildings added. It serves to give an impression of the difficulties of fighting in areas such as this. Look at the high walls, the fences and the buildings and try to imagine just how difficult it would be not only to fight through as an individual soldier, but also to try and operate as a team. Now move back to the crossroads.

The monument to 21 Independent Parachute Company on the north-west corner of the crossroads.

From the early morning of Friday 22 September 21 Independent Parachute Company dominated the area around the crossroads. They took over the area of the 'finger' with 3 Platoon at 3.00 am on Saturday 23 September, when the 10th Battalion was withdrawn. However, after suffering some heavy casualties it too was withdrawn later that day. This left the Germans free to occupy the Schoonoord. Another platoon of 21 Independent Parachute Company defended the area down

110

Pietersbergseweg as far as de Tafelberg, and yet more of them held the area of the crossroads itself. There is a monument to their presence in the garden of the house on the north-west corner of the crossroads.

It was at the crossroads that Company Sergeant Major James Steward of 21 Independent Parachute Company was approached by a German officer asking that he move back 600 metres so as to avoid risking damage to the aid station and to wounded soldiers when they, the Germans, next attacked. Given the very short distance to the western edge of the perimeter you will see that this was an impossible request which was declined and the Germans attacked elsewhere. Not every enemy soldier, however, was quite so polite, and on 24 September Private

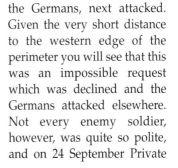

Frank Dixon reports the success of his mission to Boy Wilson. Courtesy After the Battle Magazine Film Company

Private Frank Dixon ACC taking on the German tank. This is a clip from the film Theirs is the Glory, made by veterans of the battle shortly after the war. Courtesy After the Battle Magazine Film Company

Frank Dixon of the Army Catering Corps, the company cook, was tasked by his company commander, Major Boy Wilson, to deal with a tank a little way down Utrechtseweg in the Arnhem direction, that was becoming a persistent nuisance. This he did, successfully, with a PIAT.

Walk **back towards the museum past the church** on the site of Brigadier Hackett's headquarters. **Cross ove**r J J Talsmanlaan, past the Kleyn Hartensteyn on the left and **turn down into the museum** towards the exhibit of the Sherman Tank and the 17-pounder anti-tank gun you will have seen on your visit. After a few metres you meet the junction with the path coming from the Kleyn Hartensteyn car park. Stop here, **turn right** and face the large columnar monument on the 'triangle' of ground on the other side of Utrechtseweg opposite the museum. The inhabitants of Oosterbeek presented the monument to 1st Airborne Division. General Urquhart laid the first stone in 1945 and Queen Wilhelmina of the Netherlands later unveiled the whole thing. The triangular patch of grass was the DAA from Monday 18 September to Wednesday 20 September; the place where reserves of ammunition and other supplies were held dumped on the ground. You will notice that it is open and exposed. On the far side of the triangle, beyond the monument, is a line of trees along the road that marks the western side, called Oranjeweg. This was the location of the Divisional Ordnance Field Park detachment. Comprising just four jeeps and eleven men it carried a range of spare parts. There were other RAOC soldiers managing bulk loads of stores delivered by glider and undertaking associated duties, nineteen in all.

Down the eastern side of the triangle is a narrow road adjoining Utrechtseweg almost opposite where you are standing, and called Hartensteinlaan. This was the area occupied by 250 Airborne Light Company RASC, with their headquarters in one of the houses on the northern side of the road and two platoons in the area. It was from here that Paddy Kavanagh and his men made their fateful journey to the ambush at the top of Stationsweg on 19 September.

Walk now behind the museum and from the back steps look to your half left into what is now a delightful garden of trees and shrubs. This was the area to which the ammunition and stores held in the DAA were moved on Wednesday 20 September. The open triangle of ground in front of the museum was exposed and very vulnerable to both mortar fire and snipers, and the move, inconvenient though it was, had become a practical necessity.

From the back steps of the museum you can walk down into the gardens down the path in front of you and after thirty metres take the left path which leads you to a rather battered 17-pounder anti-tank gun some 100 metres away.

The DAA, with the OFP location circled in the trees on the left and 250 Airborne Light Company on the right, where vehicles can be seen. The identity of those in the centre of the picture is unknown.
Imperial War Museum

This was the site of the artillery headquarters, and from here twenty-year old Lieutenant Paddy de Burgh kept his eye on the radio and monitored the stock levels of artillery ammunition in the DAA, which eventually occupied the area between where the gun now is and the Hartenstein. It was here, on 25 September, he took the message over the Gunner radio net: *'Op BERLIN tonight.'* Not being aware of the detail of withdrawal planning that had been underway over the

The same view today, with the memorial column in the centre of the 'green'.

Memorial column

Taken from the back steps of the museum, with the balustrade showing on the bottom left of the picture, the stores in the second DAA can be clearly seen behind the stretcher party.
Imperial War Museum

preceding twenty-four hours or so, he turned to Lieutenant Colonel Robert Loder-Symonds, the division's senior Gunner, and said: 'that means we are going, doesn't it?'

Nearby, as you move back to the museum you will see the tennis courts again, used as a cage for German prisoners of war. The prisoners incarcerated in the tennis courts were a mixed bunch, representative of the variety of units the Germans had been able to bring together to

The same view today.

counter the airborne landings. Ken Clarke, whom we last encountered at the Kavanagh ambush, was dug in nearby:

> *'I remember how mixed they were as men, some were as tired as we were, but some of the SS were very arrogant and abusive. There was a female prisoner among them and she wished to use the toilet, but no one was willing to escort her.'*

Back to the Hartenstein now, on round to its left and rejoin Utrechtseweg turning left away from Arnhem and towards the landing zones. Hoofdlaan, down which you should turn, is 200 metres on your left and fifty metres along it you will come to a house on your right: No 3. We are now entering the rear area of the 1st Battalion The Border Regiment and if you face the house you can begin to obtain a feel for the layout of the Battalion, helped by the sketch map of the area on page 121. The roundabout, which you navigated on the two previous tours, is 250 metres ahead and slightly right on Utrechtseweg, and to its left was C Company directly ahead of where you are standing. A Company is half right, and you saw their position on the last tour when we visited the '4 Brigade Hollow'. Half left, and 700 metres away, was D Company and even further round to your left, and some 1,100 to 1,300 metres away, were the two positions occupied by B Company: the Westerbouwing until Thursday 21 September and further back from then to the end of the battle on the night 25/26 September.

No 3 Hoofdlaan was the Battalion's RAP: remember, the first point at which a casualty would get to a doctor. As we go round the 1 Border

The grounds of the Hartenstein, in the background are the tennis courts where the German prisoners were kept. TAYLOR LIBRARY

Tennis courts

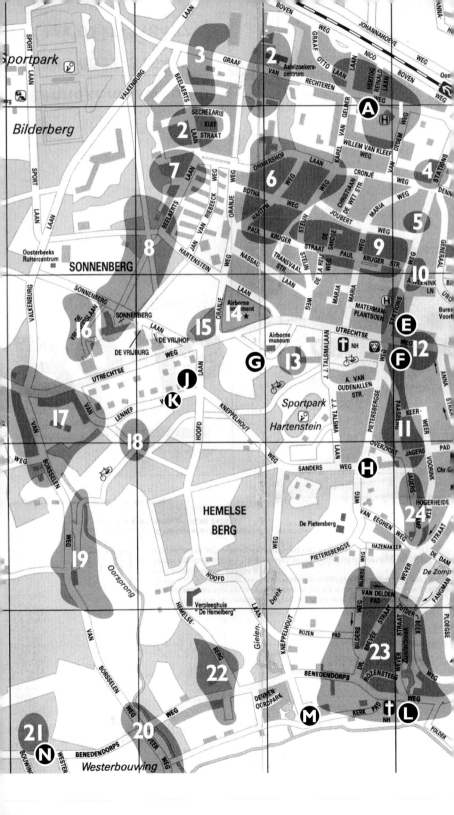

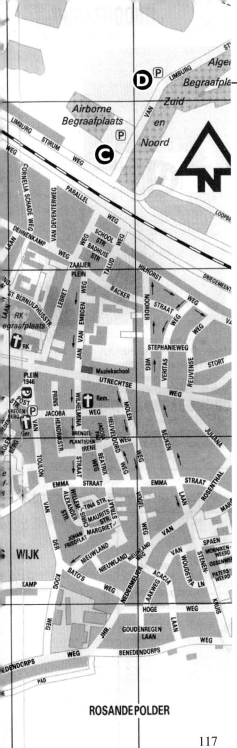

OOSTERBEEK
20-26 September 1944

KEY: A modern map of Oosterbeek is used to enable visitors to more easily identify sites and locations when visiting the area.

1. 7 KOSB to 22 Sept '44
2. 21 Ind Coy to 21 Sept '44
3. Half 4 Para Sqn to 22 Sept '44
4. Tp Recce Sqn to 22 Sept '44
5. Pl 156 Bn to 22 Sept '44
6. 7 KOSB from 22 Sept '44
7. Glider Pilots
8. A Coy 1 Border
9. 156 Bn, Glider Pilots & Recce Sqn
10. Elmn 10 Bn, Glider Pilots, Poles
11. 21 Ind Coy from 22 Sept '44
12. 10 Bn to 22 Sept '44
    3 Pl 21 Ind Coy 23 Sept '44
13. DAA from 20 Sept '44
14. DAA 18-20 Sept '44
15. HQ Recce Sqn
16. 4 Para Sqn & 9 Fd Coy RE
17. C Coy 1 Border
18. Poles from 23 Sept '44
19. D Coy 1 Border
20. Reserve Pl B Coy 1 Border
21. B Coy 1 Border
22. Breese Force
23. Lonsdale Force
24. RASC Pl

A. Hotel Dreijerord
B. Kavanagh ambush
C. CWGC Cemetery
D. Air Despatch memorial
E. Vreewijk
F. Schoonoord
G. Airborne Museum Hartenstein
H. Huis de Tafelberg
J. 1 Border RAP from 19 Sept '44
K. 1 Border Bn HQ from 19 Sept '44
L. Oosterbeek Laag Church
M. View point for evacuation route
N. Westerbouwing

**Corporal Jim McDowell is in the forground, Private Norman Knight
to the left and Private Ron Tierney is facing the centre.**
Imperial War Museum

area on this tour and on the next it is worth bearing in mind the distance
to this spot and the country through which a casualty had to be moved.
Walk on down and turn right into Van Lennepweg. After fifty metres No
3, on your right, was the Battalion HQ.

Immediately opposite that, and some fifty metres into the woods, was
the site of a 3″-mortar with its crew commanded by Corporal Jim
McDowell, with Private Norman Knight and Private Ron Tierney; and

The 6-pounder anti-tank gun being towed to its position. It was able to deal with Panzer IIIs and IVs but could only destroy a Tiger tank with a close range shot into the side.

High hedges and fencing made movement extremely difficult for the British and Germans as this picture shows. Here the men of 15 and 16 Platoons, C Company, Border Regiment, wait to repulse a German attack.

A captured mixed bunch of German soldiers, thrown together to counter the British air landings. These were taken prisoner in Wolfheze on Monday 18 September 1944. TAYLOR LIBRARY

which appears in many of the books and films about the battle. They were there to give fire support to C and D Companies in their forward positions, but so short were the ranges that the mortar was firing practically vertically in order to put the bombs where they were most needed.

Walk on along this road and it bends to the right. Stop half way between the bend and the junction with Utrechtseweg and you are at the mid-point of the area occupied by 15 and 16 Platoons of C Company, 1 Border shown in the photograph on page 119. They were in the gardens to the left and right of the road and tucked into the hedges, 15 Platoon in the area through which you have just walked, and 16 Platoon in the area up to the junction with Utrechtseweg. The other two platoons in the Company were further forward with 17 Platoon just to the left of the crossroads and 18 Platoon further south down the road to the left. On the other side of Utrechtseweg was one section of 16 Platoon protecting two Vickers machine-guns covering the area to the west and north-west and providing a link to A Company to their north. There was also a 6-pounder anti-tank gun forward in the hedge between the junction with Utrechtseweg and the Oude (Koude) Herberg crossroads.

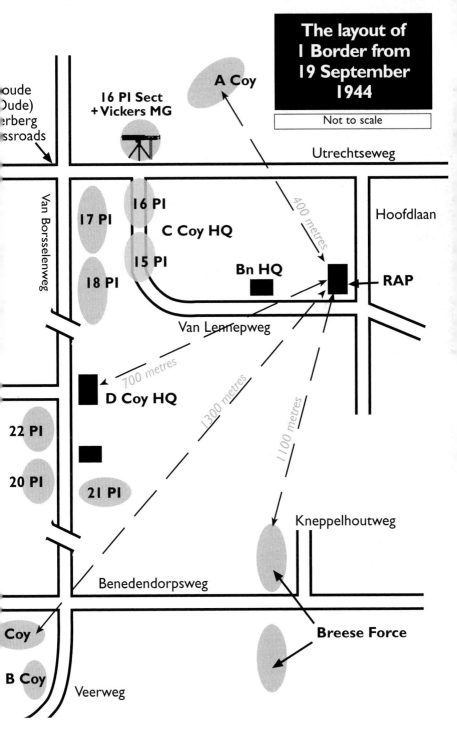

The layout of
1 Border from
19 September
1944

Not to scale

oude
(Oude)
erberg
ssroads

16 Pl Sect
+ Vickers MG

A Coy

Utrechtseweg

Van Borsselenweg

17 Pl

16 Pl

C Coy HQ

15 Pl

18 Pl

Hoofdlaan

400 metres

Bn HQ

RAP

Van Lennepweg

700 metres

D Coy HQ

1300 metres

1100 metres

22 Pl

20 Pl

21 Pl

Kneppelhoutweg

Benedendorpsweg

Breese Force

Coy

B Coy

Veerweg

121

German self-propelled guns, like the ones shown here, arrived to reinforce the circle around the beleaguered airborne forces at Oosterbeek.

That ends this short walk through part of the perimeter. Walk on up the lane; **turn right** onto the main road and return to the start point. The balance of this visit to the area will be covered in the next tour, which is best undertaken by car.

If you want a refreshment break it is always nice to do so at the café at the Westerbouwing, which you will get to in about twenty minutes on the next tour. However, it is only open daily in July and August, at weekends, by appointment for parties and infrequently otherwise. You can ring on +31 (0)263348111 to check, but depending on the time of year, therefore, you may wish to consider visiting one of the cafés near the Oosterbeek crossroads before embarking on the next part of your visit.

[1] From *Red Berets and Red Crosses* by Niall Cherry, R N Sigmond, Renkum, The Netherlands, 1999.
[2] *ibid*

CHAPTER FIVE

THE WEST, SOUTH AND EAST
OF THE PERIMETER

Duration – 1½ Hours by car
Distance – 3.6 Miles or 5.8 Kilometres

Drive from the car park and, with the trip meter at zero, proceed **west,** towards the Oude (Koude) Herberg crossroads, **turn left at the roundabout** (a recent post-war construction), trip meter **0.6 miles/1 kilometre,** and drive down Van Borsselenweg. As you make the turn you are passing the positions held by, first, 17 Platoon of C Company 1 Border and then 18 Platoon. After some 150 metres you begin to drive through an area that was unoccupied by British troops. Look to your left at the type of terrain, stopping briefly if necessary, to see how difficult it is. After about 500 metres from the crossroads you will encounter a small **turning to your right** called Wolterbeekweg, opposite a farm at No 34 Van Borsselenweg. This farm was D Company's HQ, and also housed the Company Aid Post, and they were in position on Tuesday 19 September. It may help you to refer to the map on page 121 when visiting this part of the perimeter. **Stop here.**

Recall where you saw the RAP on your walking tour, some 700 metres away in the woods from where you are now standing. Lieutenant Alan Green, commanding 20 Platoon of D Company, remembers the enormous difficulty of moving casualties over what appears such a short distance. By 20 September it was no longer possible to evacuate D Company's casualties.

The preferred method of moving casualties up Van Borsselenweg by jeep ceased to be practical and the open ground was constantly under fire from mortars and snipers preventing stretcher-bearers moving up through the woods. From 20 September wounded were cared for by the platoon medical orderlies.

One of D Company's platoons was detached to a standing patrol about a kilometre away to the south-west. With his remaining three platoons the company commander placed two in the woods on the right of the road. Responsible for Wolterbeekweg and the field to the right was 22 Platoon, and on its left 20 Platoon covered the area south and west. Just a little way further down the road is an estate-keeper's cottage and here, on its southern edge, was 21 Platoon facing south towards B Company further down Van Borsselenweg. Having driven

D Company HQ was in 34 van Borsselenweg.

this far you will now have an appreciation of the distance between companies, and will have noted the fact that C Company to the north, the nearest friendly unit, was out of sight with no chance of any kind of direct, mutual support and a huge gap through which enemy could infiltrate. The same was true of B company to the south.

The western perimeter was, really, a sieve through which the Germans should have been able to walk almost at will. It was due to the tenacity, courage and fighting capabilities of the Border Regiment

A view of 22 Platoon's area of responsibility, looking along Wolterbeekweg.

The estate keeper's cottage.

that they did not. It is perhaps worth remembering that of all the battalions involved in this battle, both in Oosterbeek and at the Bridge in Arnhem, the Border Regiment lost the most killed – 121 in all.

Having defended the area at great cost for seven days the soldiers of D Company 1 Border awoke on the morning of Tuesday 26 September to find that the Division had withdrawn and nobody had told them. Private Hugh McGuiness was there and was later to write:

'When we couldn't fight any more we just sat and waited for the Hun to come, but he still wouldn't until we told him we had no more ammunition. The SS captain asked me where my commander was. I took him to Captain Hodgson whom he saluted. Captain Hodgson was mortally wounded and could not respond. The German thanked him and us for an honourable fight; they treated us with great respect and said we were the finest soldiers they had come into combat (sic) with. When he found out how many of us were left capable of fighting he said had he known he would have taken the position two days ago.[1]'

Driel Ferry

The Driel Ferry which today is only used for foot passengers and cyclists.

Proceed on down the road to the crossroads at the bottom. Go **straight over** and you come to the Driel Ferry. Now only used for pedestrians and cycles it was, during the war, capable of taking vehicles. Pause briefly to look up at the slope of the Westerbouwing. It was from the bottom here that B Company of the 4th Battalion The Dorsetshire Regiment, with just thirty men, attacked uphill during the night of 24 September during one of the attempts by those south of the river to bring some relief to 1st Airborne Division. It is quite remarkable that fifteen of them got to the top, dislodged the Germans, who had been rolling grenades down and firing machine-guns, and held the position for a short while before being forced to surrender.

Go back to the crossroads, turn **left** up the hill and as you approach the crest you will see first the exit and then, some 50 metres further on, the entrance to the Westerbouwing café and restaurant. **Turn into the car park** and stop wherever it is convenient. If the café is open it is worth going up onto the terrace for the view, although politeness probably indicates the need to purchase something – and it is nice place for a break in your tour. The western part of the terrace is now named the 'Dorset Terrace' following a small ceremony on 20 September 2001.

Failing that, select a point half way between the terrace and the bottom of the car park and look across the Rhine to the south. Note the 'island' in the centre of the river just to the right of the line of the Driel ferry. This is a post-war river barrage, not present in 1944.

Look into the far distance across the line of the ferry and slightly to its right and you will see the chimney stacks of a power station. This is on the River Waal in Nijmegen, and indicates roughly the area from which artillery support was given, firing into the perimeter, by 64 Medium Regiment Royal Artillery from Thursday 21 September. Closer in and just across the river you can see the tower of the church in Driel. It was to the east of Driel, to the left as you look at the village, that the Polish Brigade landed on Thursday 21 September; two days late. The impact of their arrival on the Germans, however, should not be underestimated. It was further proof of the power of the Allies; it had, therefore, a significant effect on morale; and it forced the Germans to divert resources way from attacking the Oosterbeek perimeter and move forces, including armour, across the river in order to counter this new threat, thus bringing some relief to the hard-pressed airborne soldiers.

Turning now to events on the Westerbouwing. It was occupied from Tuesday 19 September to Thursday 21 September by B Company of the Border Regiment. Three platoons occupied the area across the road and around the café, rebuilt since the war following its complete destruction. They were seeking to hold any enemy advance from the west. The fourth platoon was in a depth position down the hill dug in along the small road you just drove along to get to the ferry.

The attack when it did come was ferocious. The Worrowski Battalion, part of the hastily assembled Division von Tettau, attacked at 9.00am on Thursday 21 September from the west and north-west, supported by four Renault Char B tanks from 224 Tank Company. Three of the four tanks were knocked out by PIATs, fired either by Private Ainsworth or Private Savage. On one occasion cover to fire the PIAT was taken behind a dead cow. The fourth tank withdrew. However, the German infantry pressed home their attack and after confused fighting they forced the Border Regiment soldiers off the Westerbouwing and down onto their reserve position at the bottom of the hill. Dominated by the hill, the remnants of B Company moved back deeper into the perimeter to a spot they could hold more easily and without being so exposed.

Drive out of the Westerbouwing and **turn right**, back towards the ferry crossroads and carry on straight over it. You are on the lower road and hence are driving along part of the route followed by the 2nd Battalion during its approach march on Sunday 17 September. After 400 metres you reach the corner of a wood on the left, and it was to this area that the survivors of B Company withdrew. On the right is a small

Breese Force area, former location of the gasworks on Benedendorpsweg looking south. Courtesy Drs Robert P G A Voskuil

housing estate on the site of a house called Dennenoord the cellars of which swiftly filled with casualties that could not be evacuated. There was also a gas works on the right between Dennenoord and the crossroads, which has been long since removed.

Major C F O Breese, the second-in-command of 1 Border, was ordered to take command of a mixed force comprising some men from A Company, a depleted platoon of South Staffords, some mortar-men from the 11th Battalion, and Glider Pilots. It became known as Breese Force. This makeshift force was joined by a few Poles on the night of 22/23 September, and was to remain in this area until it was withdrawn with the rest of 1st Airborne Division on the night of Monday 25/26 September. Their task was to cover the withdrawal, and then be among the last to go. On the river bank, as dawn broke on the next day, Major Charles Breese collected the remaining wounded into the last boat, whilst Sergeant Clarke led the remaining fit soldiers in swimming the river.

Proceed now along the road, named Benedendorpsweg, until you reach Dr Brevéestraat on your left, with your trip meter reading **3 Miles/4.8 kilometres. Turn left** and **immediately right** into the car park. Leave your **car and walk back** to Benedendorpsweg, **turning left** and crossing the road to the far pavement as soon as you can. You will see that you are approaching an old church, and as you do so you will be passing a large house on the right hand side, No 138. This was the home of the Ter Horst family during the war, and although it is now divided into two halves members of the Ter Horst family still live in the right hand, or western, half of the house. It is, of course, private property and a home, so due deference should be made and the Ter Horst privacy should not be disturbed by any intrusion.

The house was used from the second day to the end of the battle as the RAP for the 1st Airlanding Light Regiment whose twenty-two guns (two did not make it from the UK) were positioned in the general area of the house. Two batteries were north of Benedendorpsweg in the fields and open areas around the car park in which you have left your car. The other battery we shall see in a moment. Eventually the house became an aid station for the many wounded struck down in the area

A 75mm Gun in action.   TAYLOR LIBRARY

as the paratroopers withdrew from Arnhem, and back towards the church which marks the bottom, eastern, side of the Oosterbeek perimeter. Veterans of the battle, many of whom owe their lives to the sanctuary offered by her house, even though it was damaged in the fighting, revere Mrs Ter Horst. Along with all the citizens of the area, Mrs Ter Horst was ordered out by the Germans after the battle. Along with her five children she went to stay, with a family in the north. On her return after the war there were fifty-seven dead airborne soldiers buried in temporary graves in her garden. They have all been re-interred in the CWGC cemetery.

Walk on to the church and go round it to the far side. Here in the field on the other side of a low wall were the three guns of F Troop, half of 3 Battery 1st Airlanding Light Regiment.

The 1st Airlanding Light Regiment occupied the whole area around here, with 3 Battery here by the church and along the riverbank. Batteries had eight guns, one of F Troop's had failed to turn up, and the other two batteries were dispersed north of Benedendorpseweg, one along the line of Weverstraat immediately opposite the church and the other in the fields behind the car park in which your car is residing. Their layout is shown on the map on page 131.

On Tuesday 19 September, when attempts to reinforce 2nd

The turnstile is at the end of the track. Peter Wilkinson's HQ was on the left and E Troop's guns in the field.

Gun Positions in Oosterbeek
1st Airlanding Light Regiment

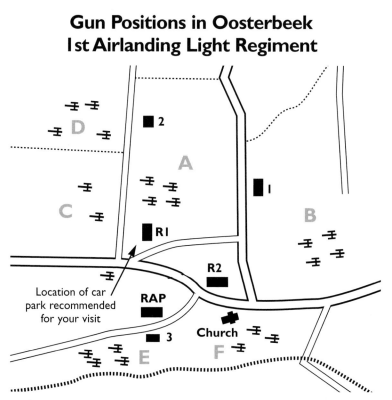

Legend:

R1 - Regimental HQ 19-21 Sept
R2 - Regimental HQ 21-25 Sept
RAP - Regimental Aid Post

Map courtesy of Peter Wilkinson MC, from his book: The Gunners at Arnhem.

Numbers **1** to **3** show the Battery HQs
Letters **A** to **F** show gun positions by troops.
There were 4 guns established per troop, 8 in a Battery; but not all the guns made the crossing from the UK.

Parachute Battalion at the bridge had failed, the remnants of 1st, 3rd and 11th Parachute Battalions and the South Staffords fought their way back towards Oosterbeek long the line of the lower road. Initially the Commanding Officer of the 1st Airlanding Light Regiment, Lieutenant Colonel 'Sherrif ' Thompson was tasked with gathering any fragments under his wing and Thompson Force was created. However, once Lieutenant Colonel Thompson was wounded the fragments were drawn together under the command of the second-in-command of the 11th Battalion, Major Dickie Lonsdale, and now became known as Lonsdale Force. Like Breese Force, a short distance away on the other side of the perimeter, it was to defend this area until the Division's withdrawal.

Look east along the direction of Benedendorpsweg at the track 100 metres away which turns to the right of the road just on a bend opposite a garage. Soldiers of 1st and 3rd Battalions were dug in here along the line of the track down towards the river, with the remnants of 11th Battalion in the houses around the garage. Almost opposite the church is Weverstraat, and some 200 metres this road the South Staffords defended the area east of Weverstraat. G Squadron of the Glider Pilot Regiment defended the gun areas and occupied the houses to the north of the laundry, and there were some thirty soldiers in the fields south of the church facing the river.

Lieutenant Michael Dauncey of the Glider Pilot Regiment was with G Squadron of his regiment and was involved in the defence of this area from 20 September to 25 September. German armoured vehicles supported by infantry attacked his position continually, and there were occasions when they prevailed and overran the British defended localities. Lieutenant Dauncey was instrumental in leading the counter-attacks that evicted them; counter-attacks that he organised on his own initiative. He also made a practice of assaulting enemy machine-gun positions with great success, and continued to do so despite having been wounded three times.

It was during a particularly heavy attack on 24 September, supported by tanks and by self-propelled guns, that he was wounded again, losing this time the sight of one eye. Even this did not stop him, and such was the force of the attack he led against the Germans, despite the pain he was in and the loss of vision, that they were beaten back and the lost ground recovered. Artillery fire from 64 Medium Regiment in Nijmegen played a major part in repelling the German assault, which otherwise might easily have cut the Division off from the river.

On 25 September, the last day before withdrawal across the river, his position was once again subjected to intense fire from an enemy self-propelled gun. The houses being occupied by his men were set on fire and he was ordered to withdraw. There were no anti-tank weapons left, and within just a few moments there was every likelihood that the enemy would be able to get inside the gun positions, whereupon they would have been able to wreak real havoc upon the crucially important guns and the Division would have been denied their very important support. Michael Dauncey clearly did not consider this to be sensible, and being alone he single-handedly attacked the mobile gun using a Gammon Bomb.

The Gammon Bomb comprised a small stockingette bag into which was stuffed plastic explosive. A fuze, known as the 'Always' fuze, and

The Germans used armoured vehicles such as this StuG self-propelled gun to fire into houses and flush out paratroopers for German patrols to hunt down.

numbered in the Army inventory Fuze No 69, was attached. It was designed such that the plastic explosive would be smacked onto the tank's armour, rather like a sort of 'cow pat', and then detonated, whereupon the shock-wave of the detonation would pass through the armour and detach a 'scab' of steel off the far side about the same size as the 'pat'. This chunk of metal would then whizz round inside the tank, white hot, at great speed and accompanied by shards of steel from the edges of the 'scab', to the acute discomfort of the inhabitants of the armoured vehicle.

It was Heath Robinson, but effective. The only problem was that the man who launched it had to get very close indeed to his target. It was, to say the least, a hazardous business. Michael Dauncey, half blind, four times wounded, exhausted, under-fed and probably quite cross, was successful in thwarting this attack, but in the process was injured yet again and was captured by the Germans. He eventually managed to escape from hospital in December 1944 and made his own way to British lines. He was recommended for the Victoria Cross and was awarded the Distinguished Service Order for his bravery, and eventually retired from a post-war Army career as a Brigadier.

Major Bill Chidgey RAOC. Collection F R Steer

Walk along the south side of the church and you will see a footpath running along the rear of the Ter Horst House. Follow it through a metal turnstile and in the field on your left were the four guns of E Troop 3rd Battery. The battery's Command Post Officer, Lieutenant Peter Wilkinson, was positioned in a house just to the east of the one near the turnstile, but which was never rebuilt having been extensively damaged. **Walk on for another 100 metres** or so beyond the turnstile to a point where the footpath crosses another coming down from the farmhouses to your right towards the stream and the river forelands to your left. This is a good point from which to view the crossing area.

When it was felt that the 1st Airborne Division could hold on no longer and that relief by forces approaching from the south was not a practical option it was decided to evacuate the Division. This took place on the night of 25/26 September 1944. Major General Urquhart's plan for the withdrawal was to collapse the perimeter into the centre of the position, leaving wounded in place firing weapons to delude the enemy. Radio messages would also continue to be sent for the same purpose. Doctors, medical orderlies and padres were to remain with the wounded. Glider Pilots were to mark two routes and Benedendorpsweg was to be the start line. If, in fact, two routes were marked they were certainly not used by everybody. Many survivors of the battle speak of moving towards the river, but not following a marked path. Down through the area where you are standing part of the Division moved to the river, the sound of their progress being muffled by the sacking they had tied round their boots and by the terrible rain and wind that whipped up that evening, to where they would be ferried across the river by Royal Engineers and Royal Canadian Engineers in canvas boats. From the south side of the river Bofors 40mm anti-aircraft cannon fired tracer along two lines to show the boundaries outside which they should not stray. From Nijmegen, 64 Medium Regiment together with other XXX Corps artillery bombarded German positions and targets near to the perimeter.

Knowing that something was afoot, but not sure if it was a reinforcement, the Germans, who did not enjoy operating at night, stepped up their activity. Over near the church, which you can see from where you are standing, a party of KOSB had a run-in with some Germans, but beat them off. This is a clear example of how close were the enemy and shows yet again how narrow was the area into which the Division was crammed.

Elsewhere random fire into the perimeter created difficulties for those trying to make their way to the crossings. Major Bill Chidgey, the Officer Commanding the Ordnance Field Park, was one of those:

'The tape-marked route petered out after a few yards. I was on the left flank... Entering a small copse we met opposing fire and decided we should bear left away from it. After some fifty yards or so we ran into immense heavy machine gun fire. I told Sergeant Bennett to withdraw those he could and make his way further left to the river whilst we would help by delaying the enemy. After about half and hour, during which time we were pinned down, the three forward sections eased their way to the left with the intent of following the rear section down to the river. This was not to be as the enemy had closed the gap... on my right I heard a thump and a gasp which told me... had been hit and, by his silence, was killed instantly. There were other sounds of casualties in our group. I felt two hits, one in each shoulder and a searing pain in my back. I passed out. When I came to I found I was unable to move my legs, but there had been plenty of noise and disturbance around for our own artillery had been giving covering fire for the withdrawal and shells had landed on our position. The next morning at daylight... there was no way out. I couldn't move and the men had suffered casualties. We jettisoned the firing mechanisms of our weapons and accepted the inevitable.'

Private Sydney Harsley RAOC, one of Bill Chidgey's soldiers, was luckier:

'I was on my own and saw people moving away from the area

Sergeant N G 'Bill' Griffin RASC.
Collection F R Steer

and so I followed. I ended up near a gas works where there was an upturned dinghy. There were three or four other blokes there. We turned it the right way up and using our rifles as paddles made our way across the river.'

Lieutenant Paddy de Burgh was moving towards the river with two of his soldiers when one was killed by a burst of machine-gun fire and the other wounded, his left hand being almost severed. Paddy took him to an aid station that was by then occupied by Germans where he was 'invited to stay.' The following morning, however, he managed to escape the attentions of his captors and made his way down to the river. Clad only in gym shoes and underpants he swam to the other side, being fired on by a machine-gun from somewhere on the north bank. Eventually reaching a groin jutting out into the river on the far bank he sheltered until the German machine-gunner found something else to shoot at. Walking up the dyke he found a Royal Canadian Engineer sentry asleep by his Bren gun. Having tapped the man on the head and asked him what he thought he would do if he, Paddy, had been a German, he left the surprised, but by now very much awake, Canadian soldier and, having been given battledress to wear, walked to Nijmegen. On arrival he asked for the opportunity for just three hours sleep, and slept for twenty-seven.

Some soldiers chose to swim during the night rather than wait for a space on a boat. Some were unsuccessful, and Lance Corporal Hughes of the RASC remembers a friend who did not make it:

'It was a terrific shock to me... to find out the number of my pals who had not returned. Amongst these was the lad who had been with me ever since we first volunteered for parachuting. We did our first jump together, Legs Wattam. His name, though, still lives in the memory of all those that returned – and we still, especially on *exercises, find it hard to realise he is not with us. He was last seen swimming the Rhine – but his chances were little of reaching the other bank.'*

Many who drowned are interred in civilian cemeteries to the west, downstream, of Oosterbeek. There was also a case of one soldier who survived the swim, but on exiting the river found he had gone in a circle and was back where he had started.

Having crossed the river men made their way to Nijmegen where reception facilities were being put in place. Instrumental in doing this were the men in the Seaborne Echelon, desperate to help where they could and to discover information about their friends and colleagues who had been fighting north of the river. Some walked, and others managed to get lifts. Major Geoffrey Powell of 156 Parachute Battalion formed the remnants of his unit into a squad and marched them away; just fifteen strong. Bill Griffin was luckier, but his journey was not without its moments:

'We were told that if a man was wounded he was to be left behind. It was my twenty-first birthday, and I thought, "Today I'm going to die". I never thought I'd see my twenty-first birthday out. Three of the divisional headquarters clerks got out: Me, Corporal Daniel Lewis and Lance Corporal Norman Davis. I got out in a Canadian boat. We couldn't start the engine and it was drifting down the river before we eventually got it going. Having got over I headed for a Dorset soup kitchen. Heading back from the river in a DUKW it slipped into a dyke and we all ended up in the ditch, but the driver got it out and drove us to Nijmegen.'

Some even had work to do shortly after they reached the other side, as Sergeant J L Lambert of the Army Catering Corps attached to 156 Parachute Battalion explained:

'I recollect crossing enemy lines with the Colour Sergeant to get the password for withdrawal into the divisional perimeter, and then the incredible calm of our eventual withdrawal across the river to find tea on the other side. Then finally back to England ahead of the main body to fix up "grub" on arrival with only two of my para cooks left. Quite a business, this Army cooking!'

Ken Clarke made it to the river during the night and fell asleep on the open ground waiting his turn to cross. He was woken at 4.00 am in time to catch one of the last boats. By first light it was over. Just 2,135 of the 10,005 men of 1st Airborne Division had escaped. The remainder were either dead, wounded or missing; and while some were to escape in the ensuing months they were few in number.

Sergeant Bill Chedgey (right) RASC.
Collection F R Steer

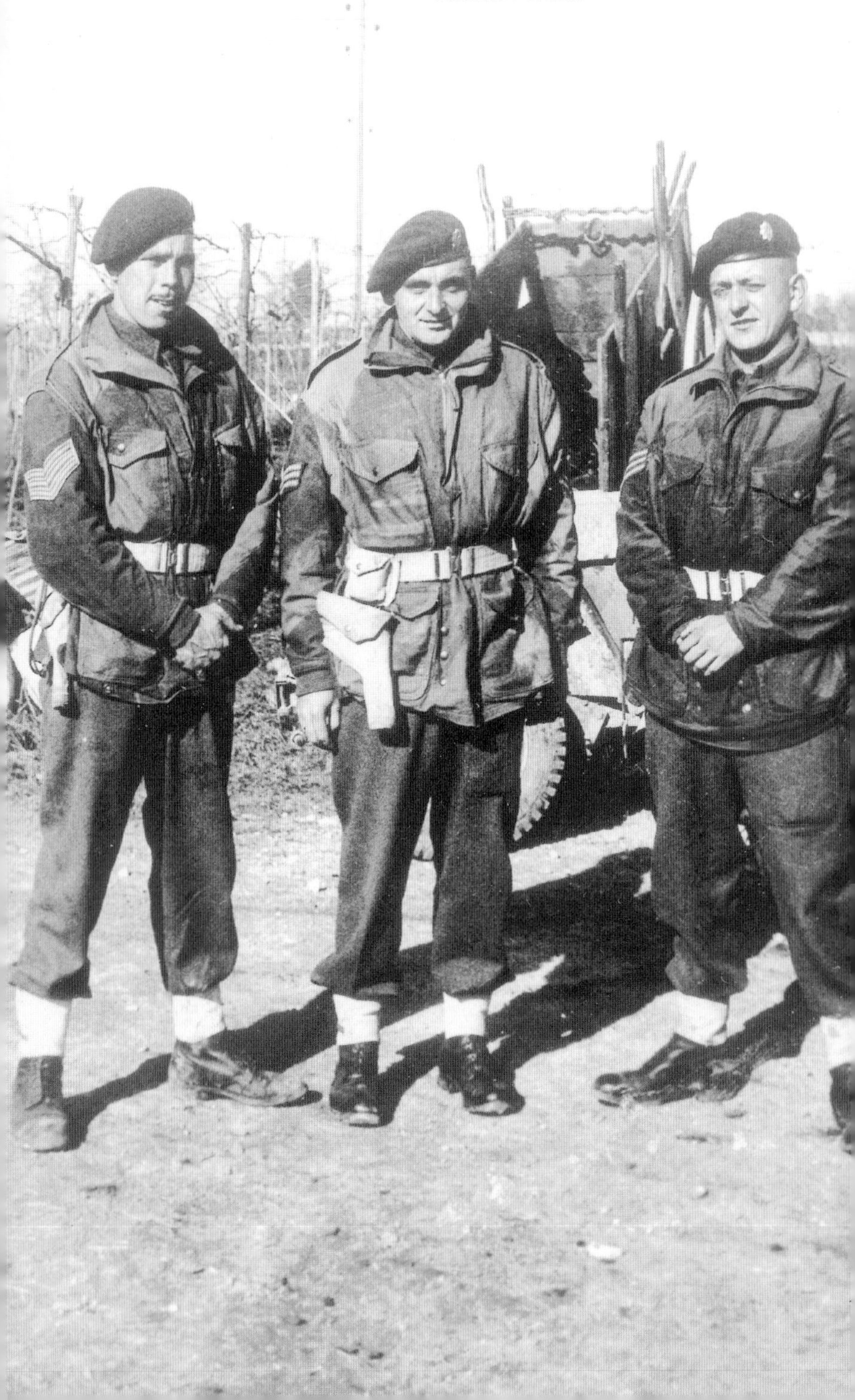

Walk back to your car, leave the car park and **turn left** onto Benedendorpsweg and then up Weverstraat. You are now driving up the eastern perimeter. The early part of the drive takes you through the area occupied first by the South Staffords and G Squadron of the Glider Pilots. On reaching the junction with Van Eeghenweg and Jagerskamp you enter the area into which a Royal Army Service Corps platoon was positioned from 22 September.

Some forty strong, and commanded by Captain Jack Cranmer-Byng, it was a composite organisation made up from the survivors of 250 Airborne Light Company less the few required to continue managing the very limited stocks left in the DAA. The fighting here was hard with constant probes by the Germans seeking to test and penetrate the airborne hold on the perimeter and the paratroopers fighting back tenaciously.

Sergeant Bill Chedgey was part of Jack Cranmer-Byng's force, and he was in a house near the bottom end of Jagerskamp. From upstairs in one of the buildings he saw a German patrol, and tapping his Bren gunner on the shoulder he directed him onto his target. A few well-aimed bursts killed a number of the enemy, whilst others were wounded and the balance fled. Bill, realising that he was now a target and expecting the Germans to bring up a tank or a self-propelled artillery piece, led his men out of the house and went back towards Cranmer-Byng's headquarters deeper into the perimeter. The use of a self-propelled gun or tank against buildings had become a standard tactic to drive the defenders out into the open. Once they were clear of

A German patrol moves with caution as they look for British paratroopers.

An example of a German mortar team in action.

the protection offered by the buildings the airborne soldiers would then be hunted down by the Germans using mortar fire. However, on this occasion Bill and his men were able to escape unscathed and made it back to the headquarters, where they were able to rest.

However, much against his better judgement, he was back the next day with his men, certain that SP guns would target his building. What followed, though, was a period, almost the whole day, of virtually complete inactivity. This alarmed Bill, and he said so, believing it to be the lull before a storm and that to remain in the position was foolish. Eventually, the expected self-propelled gun arrived – the storm was about to materialise. Sergeant Chedgey dashed upstairs into the front bedroom for a look, and as he did so the gun fired two rounds into the house. Bill was blown over, tumbling over and over as he fell down the stairs, to end up at the bottom with a broken femur. In great pain, he was left with very few options. Clearly the house was no longer a tenable position, for they had nothing with which to defeat the powerful armoured vehicle pitted against them. It could quite simply stand off and blow the building, with them in it, to pieces.

He ordered his men to withdraw, and watched as they raced back

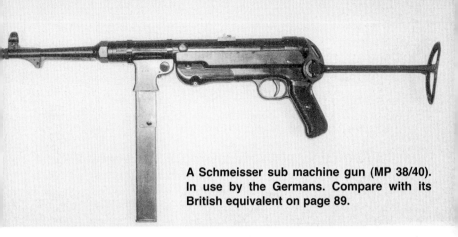

A Schmeisser sub machine gun (MP 38/40). In use by the Germans. Compare with its British equivalent on page 89.

across the fields. Some were killed as the German mortars tracked them down, whilst others managed to escape to some relative form of safety in the woods beyond the houses. Discarding his two phosphorous grenades and his two Mills grenades, Bill awaited capture as he lay in pain in the hallway of the house. Soon the barrel of a *Schmeisser* sub-machine gun was poked into his stomach, and in German he was asked by one of four youngsters where his comrades were. Speaking a little German, he responded that they had gone. Unsure about what to do with their captive, the sixteen to eighteen year old Germans were faced with an injured sergeant. In their world, his equivalent, a *feldwebel*, was God, and Bill was treated accordingly. Before long they had constructed a stretcher, had made the sergeant as comfortable as they could and carted him off to hospital.

Moving on up Jagerskamp you come to the houses occupied by, among others, Driver Ron Pearce:

'We were part of the brigade defences under Captain Cranmer-Byng. I was in 16 Jagerskamp with three others, and next door in 18 there were about twelve of us. It had been very quiet for some time, and the rest said there was no point in staying so they went back to the Hartenstein. We decided to stay in our house, those were our orders. Suddenly, there were a load of Germans coming up the street. I shouted to the Lance Corporal who rushed out to tackle them and was shot in the doorway. They surrounded the house, and fired a Panzerfaust *into the house. I was with John Prime, who had learned some German in Italy. Surrounded and with no chance of escape or of doing anything productive we had no choice but to*

The German Panzerfaust was a shoulder-controlled anti-tank weapon capable of penetrating 200mm of armour plate.

Achtung ! Feuerstrahl !

surrender, and so he called out in German. They came to the foot of the stairs and called us down.'

Turning left onto Overzicht you reach the junction with Pietersbergseweg and as you turn right towards the Oosterbeek crossroads a glance to your left will show you the Tafelberg.

As you make your way home, or to your hotel or camp site you may wish to reflect briefly on what you have read and seen and give thanks for the fact that men such as those who landed here in The Netherlands in 1944 were there when we needed them at a time of great danger for our homes, our families, our safety and, not least, our way of life; and pray that we do not need young men like them to make the same sacrifices again. Think also of the Dutch who they came to liberate, and marvel at the affection and esteem they have for the airborne soldiers who landed here despite the loss of life, the devastation and the subsequent German evacuation and looting of the entire area. Ask them why and they will tell you that it is because they tried, and to a people in the grip of a tyrant that meant everything.

Of course, having completed your tour of the landing zones and Oosterbeek there is still the Bridge in Arnhem and the approaches to it for you to discover; but that will have to be for another day.

[1] From *When Dragons Flew* by Stuart Eastwood, Charles Gray and Alan Green, The Regimental Museum The Border Regiment in association with Silver Link Publishing Ltd, Peterborough 1994.

INDEX

143

144